memphis

memphis

Objects, Furniture, and Patterns

Richard Horn

A QUARTO BOOK

RUNNING PRESS
BOOK PUBLISHERS
PHILADELPHIA, PENNSYLVANIA

A RUNNING PRESS/QUARTO BOOK

9 8 7 6 5 4 3 2 1

Digit on the right indicates the number of this printing

Library of Congress Cataloging in Publication Number
84–042924

ISBN 0-89471-307-8

MEMPHIS: Objects, Furniture, and Patterns
was prepared and produced by
Quarto Marketing Ltd.
15 West 26th Street, New York, N.Y. 10010

Editor: Naomi Black
Art Director: Richard Boddy
Designer: Rod Gonzalez
Photo Researcher: Susan Duane
U.K. Photo Researcher: Sylvia Katz

Typeset by BPE Graphics, Inc.
Color separations by Hong Kong
Scanner Craft Company Ltd.
Printed and bound in The Netherlands by Comproject
b.v. Holland

JACKET PHOTO CREDITS

Front: Ettore Sottsass, Jr., "Letraset" pattern, 1983
(Courtesy of Artemide)
Michele de Lucchi, "Lido" sofa (Courtesy of The Design
Council—London)

Back, from top, clockwise: Andrea Branzi, "Century"
dormeuse, 1982 (Courtesy of Janus Gallery)
Ettore Sottsass, Jr., "Euphrates" vase, 1983 (Courtesy of
Artemide)
Peter Shire, "Bel Air" chair, 1982 (Courtesy of Artemide)

This book may be ordered from the publisher
Please include $1.00 postage
(But try your bookstore first.)

Running Press Book Publishers
125 South 22nd Street
Philadelphia, Pennsylvania 19103

ABOUT THE AUTHOR

Richard Horn is a novelist and journalist specializing in design and architecture. His articles have appeared in such publications as The Home Section of *The New York Times, Architectural Digest, New York, Art & Antiques, Metropolitan Home, Industrial Design,* and the Italian design magazines *Gran Bazaar* and *FMR*. He has also published DESIGNS (1981), a playful *roman à clef* about the New York design scene. A graduate of Columbia College and a Kellett Fellow, he is currently a senior editor of *House Beautiful's Home Decorating* and is at work on a book about American designs of the 1950s.

contents

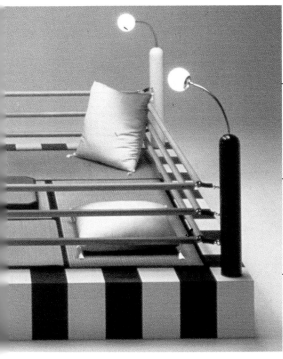

AFTER MODERNISM, WHAT?

I t is never easy to predict the location of the holes in the net of design history. For reasons not always fathomable, some styles are caught by that net, and they stay with us. Other styles fall through the holes, and keep on falling, right into oblivion. Occasionally, though, some styles are retrieved and brought back as if brand new to delight, intrigue, and spur us on in unforeseen directions.

Since its founding in 1981, Memphis, the contemporary Italian design movement, has accomplished just such a retrieval. Up until then, Modern design reigned supreme. Bauhaus imperatives of form and functionality prevailed not only in Italy but throughout Europe and the United States as well. The contemporary furniture available to us—those pieces that furniture manufacturers viewed as profitable to produce and that the decorating magazines and interior designers touted—was *Modern:* cool, spare, clean-lined, and wholly lacking in pattern and ornament. The colors of these pieces were most often neutral, with an occasional primary. Quite apart from its visual appearance, this furniture was functional. Yet it maintained a pure, rigidly puritanical and dead-serious quality that, by the early 1960s, was being questioned.

In the United States, architect Robert Venturi started that questioning with his "gentle manifesto" of 1962, *Complexity and Contradiction in Architecture.* "I am for messy vitality over obvious unity," he wrote in that influential book. "I include the *non sequitur* and proclaim the duality." Later, in *Learning from Las Vegas* (1972), Venturi, Denise Scott Brown, and Steven Izenour argued not only for a complex and contradictory architecture but also for what they termed "the decorated shed"—that is, "architecture as shelter with symbols on it." In calling for a reevaluation of architectural ambiguity and ornamentation, these architects were protesting the hard-edged, unornamented buildings (and, by implication, furniture) that epitomized the Modern style.

By the early 1960s, however, Modern was considered the only suitable style for the postwar world. As its status grew, styles from the past—particularly those current during the *fin de siècle* and early years of the twentieth century—started falling through the net. Indeed, these

With this interior (left) Ettore Sottsass suggests how elements of Memphis can make a coherent interior design. The look is at once austere and high-spirited. American furniture designer and artist Tom Loeser designed a chest of drawers (right) built with wood and Colorcore. Its bright, enameled-on tones and highly eccentric form show a certain Memphis touch—with a definite American flavor.

If a Memphis designer limits himself or herself to a single color, chances are that the form a piece takes will be extravagant. This is clearly true in Matteo Thun's porcelain vases "Titaca" and "Onega." The superb workmanship of these pieces contrasts amusingly with their outrageous, flat cartoonish shapes and lines.

Gerard Taylor's "Le Palme," made of metal, glass, and plastic laminate, is one of Memphis' more straightforward storage pieces. Although it sticks to the basic idea of what a bookcase or étagère "should" be, its unusual colors and asymmetrical configuration bring elements of freshness and surprise to what, in less adventurous designs, would be no more than a monochromatic, rectilinear storage piece. This could easily fit into any number of rooms—from a large, modern bathroom to a more traditional bedroom.

styles—including the work of the Glasgow School, the Art Nouveau and *Jugendstil* designers, the Wiener Werkstaette, the Catalan visionary architect Antonio Gaudí, as well as that of numerous others—had been headed for design oblivion since the 1920s. All had been inspired by the English Arts and Crafts movement which, starting in the 1860s, had called for a return to handicrafts and quality in the face of rapidly increasing mechanization and the mass production of shoddy, unattractive furniture and objects. As an alternative, they created complex, decorative, and often densely symbolic objects (many of them costly and made in small quantities) and buildings which, while never acquiring wide popularity, were highly successful in their own right.

Amid the devastation of World War I, however, these Arts-and-Crafts-inspired design movements were quickly forgotten. Handicrafts seemed more than ever a thing of the past, and no one wanted to dwell on the past just then. The future, however, held great promise—a promise embodied, so far as certain architects and designers were concerned, by industry and mass production, the very things the Arts and Crafts designers had opposed.

Many designers who had been producing decorative objects and furniture before the War did, in fact, survive it. However, their work was now viewed as passé and out of keeping with the new postwar spirit. That spirit demanded fresh beginnings in design and architecture. The fantastic, colorful, richly ornamented, and idiosyncratic buildings, furniture, textiles, wallpapers, and accessories of the early twentieth century were seen as irrelevant. What was needed was something as rational, uncluttered, and pure as life itself would become in Europe after the "war to end all wars."

The answer to this urgent need—Modern design—was developed at the Bauhaus, particularly in the late 1920s and early 1930s, and in France by Le Corbusier. Unlike the pre-1914 decorative designs, Modern designs were spare and geometrical. Function and the technologies of mass production determined form. Symbolism, pattern, and ornamentation were eliminated, as were all references to past styles. Indeed, as was only fitting for the fresh start Europeans wanted to make, Modern design seemed totally ahistorical, to have emerged from out of nowhere—an absolutely fresh start in and of itself.

Looking back, we can see that Modern design did not make life in Europe as rational as many had hoped. Nor, after World War II had run its course and Europe lay in ruins once more, did Modern design transform the United States. This transatlantic importation was largely due to the movement's leading practitioners, among them Marcel Breuer, Walter Gropius, Laszlo and Sibyl Moholy-Nagy, and Ludwig Mies van der Rohe. America had emerged victorious from World War II, and so a style change seemed in order there, not so much to provide

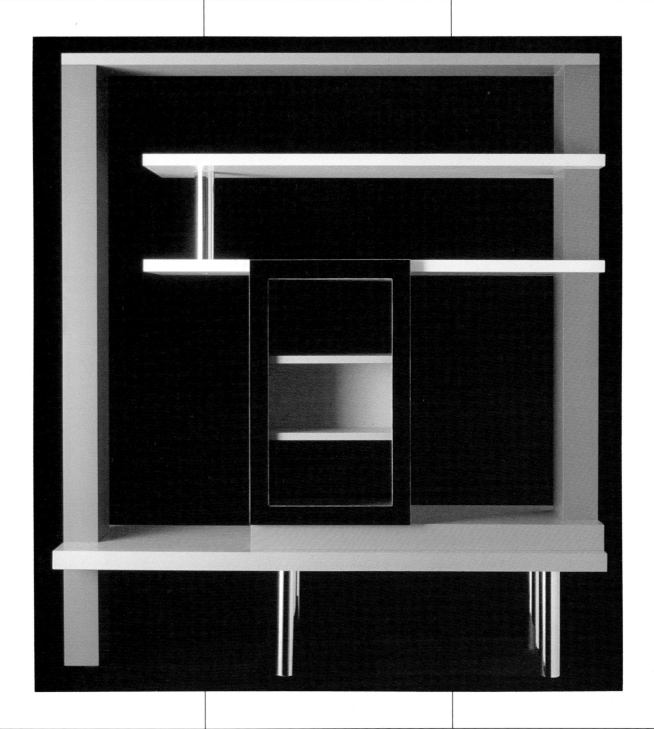

the setting for a rationalistic utopia but to celebrate what had become the most powerful nation on earth. One outcome of this, Modern-style buildings, became symbols of burgeoning corporate power.

Italy had lost World War II. Yet somehow, the Modern style struck Italian designers as appropriate for their country too, if for different reasons. Modernism provided a formula according to which simple, rational designs could be created for what postwar Italy hoped would be a simpler, more rational time—a hope similar to that which gave rise to Modern design in the first place. But while Americans were erecting new skyscrapers, Italian designers, stymied by the shambles of the postwar Italian building industry, turned their attention to furniture. Design philosophies varied from one group of designers to the next, though most agreed that handcrafted, ornamented designs were not appropriate for the time.

Throughout the fifties, sixties, and seventies, Modern design developed apace in both Italy and America. And yet, at the same time, a counterstyle was taking shape that could be described as an exaggerated, picturesque Modernism, full of exuberant colors and bizarre but dynamic forms. This was Pop—the style of the postwar suburbs that celebrated the new Atomic Age in its own rambunctious way. Most "serious" architects dismissed Pop as mindless kitsch, but the postwar world was too big and complex for any one mode of architectural thinking to wholly prevail. And so Pop went its own way, more or less unaware that architecture's grand pooh-bahs had deemed it tasteless.

With the postwar communications boom, the West rediscovered the East and, especially in the 1960s, embraced it. The modern glass-and-steel aesthetic continued to enjoy prestige in large Western cities, but it was not about to erase the rich Eastern and African design traditions that the hippies and black liberationists were exploring along with other non-Western ways of living. Nor would that rigid aesthetic have made much sense to those who experimented with mind-expanding drugs and saw that there was more to existence than the rational grid that Western capitalist civilization had laid over it.

By the mid-seventies, however, all these exuberant reevaluations of life had run out of steam. Modernism, both in Europe and America, remained if not entirely unquestioned, at least secure in its role of "Leading Design Philosophy of the World." Revolutionary in the 1920s, Modern design was now big business. Big corporations bought it. Big manufacturers produced it. Large numbers of people used it to furnish their homes. Consequently, many designers kept on designing it. To

The Grace Designs showroom in Dallas was designed by Sottsass Associati, the studio headed by Ettore Sottsass. It provides Americans with their first opportunity to see Memphis furniture in a setting created by the same designers who created the pieces themselves.

Vernon Reed calls "Hyperspace" an "electronic neckpiece." Designed in 1984, it measures 6 inches by 9 inches with its neckring. Its decidedly space-age materials include anodized titanium, acrylic, electroplated brass, rubber, and electronic circuitry. Its pattern of asymmetrical shapes and vaguely ritualistic character (it looks like an adornment that a priest or priestess might wear) recall Memphis motifs.

Carmen Spera's use of oddly combined colors and quirky forms in his "Capri" bar (right) has much in common with Memphis pieces, although Spera, a New Yorker associated with the path-blazing gallery Art et Industrie, actually arrived at his particular style of design on his own. Known especially for his handpainted finishes, Spera diverges from Memphis in his more craftsmanlike approach. Memphis finishes, on the other hand, tend to be no more than plastic laminates and are printed by machine.

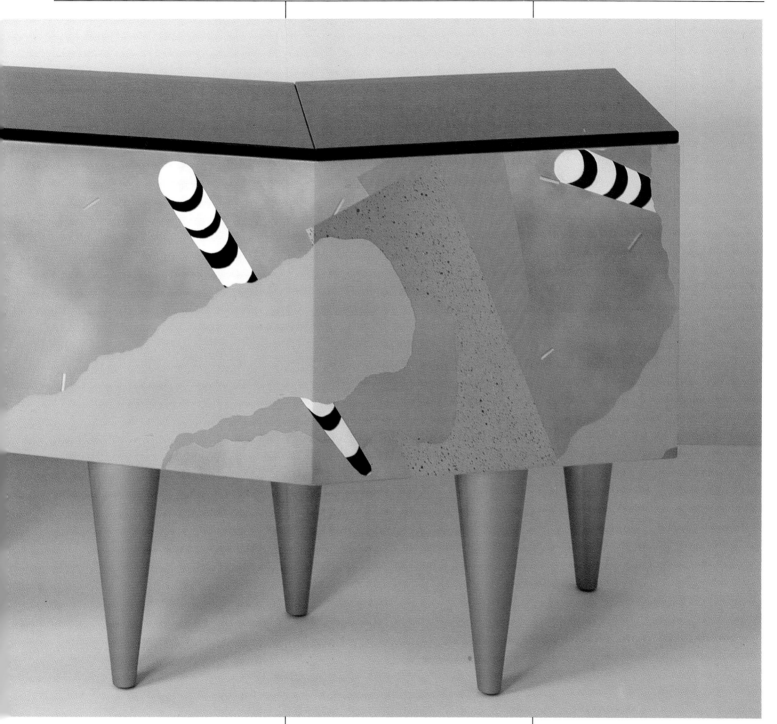

them, the hippie movement seemed unimportant. Inflation set in, prices rose, and cost-efficient mass-production possibilities ruled all thinking in the design field. The Arts and Crafts tradition of decorative, handcrafted objects seemed less relevant than ever. And while non-Western design and craft traditions were studied in universities, rarely did they influence what showed up on the marketplace. Sensing the country's growing conservatism, the American furniture industry devoted most of its energies to churning out reproductions and adaptations of pre-1900 American styles. At the same time, Italy's Modern furniture and lighting became known throughout the world for their sleek allure. All through the 1970s, its leading role in the home furnishings field remained uncontested.

AFTER MODERNISM, THIS

Just as in America Robert Venturi and his associates had called for a richer, more complex and symbolic architecture, in Italy there was an architect who also worked as a designer, artist, and craftsperson—and who was also interested in enriching objects rather than in making them simpler, purer, and more functional. Born in Austria in 1917, Ettore Sottsass, Jr. was trained as an architect, but first made his mark in the late fifties as an industrial designer for Olivetti. Along with this lucrative "straight" work, however, Sottsass also explored his own wide-ranging interests, particularly oriental mysticism, which led to the creation of fanciful, symbolic, and overtly playful artworks, furniture, plastics, ceramics, metalware, jewelry, tapestries, and lighting.

Underlying these experiments, from the mid-sixties on, was Sottsass' interest in areas of design that lay outside Modernism's domain (within which his own functional designs for Olivetti would have to be included): Eastern and Third World traditions; the Pop style of suburbia; and the Arts-and-Crafts-inspired European decorative designs of the early twentieth century. This constellation of interests, already apparent by the mid-1960s, ultimately led to the founding of Memphis in 1981.

Sottsass was far from alone in his dissatisfaction with Modern design. During the sixties, several Milanese designers and architects experimented with a wide variety of unusual concepts for shelter and home living. Some maintained that to undo the status quo, all traditional notions of shelter had to be radically (if whimsically) transformed. Others, less extreme, created prototype living environments which, though never mass-produced, proved quite thought-provoking.

Memphis' 1982 collection "Altair," a glass piece designed by Ettore Sottsass. Note the mischievous placement of handles and other excrescences.

STUDIO ALCHYMIA

This rash of experimentation died down by the early 1970s. But with the founding of Studio Alchymia in Milan in the late seventies by Sottsass and fellow architect-designers Andrea Branzi, Michele de Lucchi, Alessandro Mendini, and Paola Navone, another alternative to Modernism, dubbed "Il Nuovo Design," came into existence.

Studio Alchymia's designs were odd and unexpected. They owed nothing to Modern design. The forms of these lamps, tables, sofas, chairs, storage pieces, and objects of undetermined function were at once exuberant and arbitrary. Compared to Modern design's neutral

Ettore Sottsass' "Park Lane" coffee table is made of the unlikely combination of fiberglass and marble. By juxtaposing an expensive material and an inexpensive material, Sottsass tries to laugh off the hierarchies of powerful and powerless by which most societies are organized. Apart from the political content of such a design, this piece also boasts undeniable eye-appeal along with an unusual combination of colors.

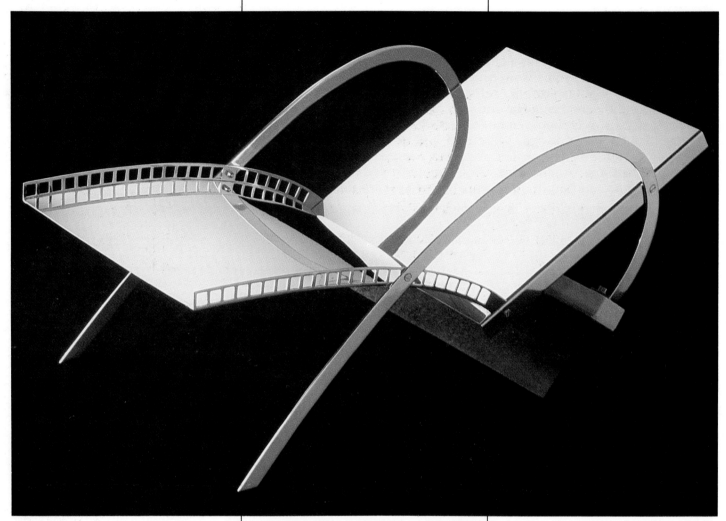

The "Bering" fruitbowl, designed by Matteo Thun, was featured in Memphis' 1982 collection. Made of marble and silver, it defies mass-production concerns for marketability and the bottom line with its frankly expensive and elitist materials. Its border of pierced squares recalls another design movement that favored rich materials and handcrafting: the Wiener Werkstaette, where this motif was used on a variety of objects.

palette, the colors were audacious—everything from obscenely creamy pastels to intentionally ugly tans to brilliant acid greens and glittery blues and reds. Materials, too, were most surprising, particularly the preponderance of patterned plastic laminates, and the sort of speckled metal flake finishes seen more often on accordions or electric guitars than on pieces of furniture by well-known and well-respected designers. Unlike the mass-produced Modern Italian design that had become highly successful throughout the world, Studio Alchymia's strikingly individualistic pieces were—like the decorative designs of the early twentieth century—handcrafted and produced in very small quantities. This constituted a reaction to the limitations and repetitiveness of mass production, as well as to an impatience with questions of marketability and ergonomics—engineering and design dictated by the contours and functioning of the human body.

In addition to creating curious-looking objects that ran counter to the Italian norm, the Studio Alchymia designers participated in performance events and left-wing politics and issued numerous manifestos stating their case. Among their most articulate spokesmen was Andrea Branzi. In a 1981 issue of the Italian design magazine *Modo*, Branzi established the aims of Il Nuovo Design: "1) Putting behind the myth of the 'unity' of a project and concentrating on a free discontinuity of parts with respect to the whole. 2) The search for a new linguistic 'expressive' quality as a possible solution to the enigma of design and as a possible new meaning. 3) Recycling all possible idioms now in circulation within the experience of our lives. 4) Recuperating decoration and color as signs of freedom and nobility of creative invention. 5) Going beyond ergonomic limits and concentrating on an affective relationship between man and his things."

ENTER MEMPHIS

Branzi's stated aims still pertain to what eventually became Memphis. However, Studio Alchymia proved less than viable financially, and perhaps a bit too politically adventurous to suit possible investors. Indeed, sizeable financial backing for such avant-garde furniture was not forthcoming until 1981, when a number of Italian manufacturers decided to back Memphis—an enterprise which, like Studio Alchymia, was initially removed from the contingencies and aims of mass production and which therefore did not seem to promise much in the way of profits.

Pieces for what turned out to be the first collection in 1981 were designed by Sottsass (who emerged as the new concern's leading light and was instrumental in its inception); by his associates, Matteo Thun, Marco Zanini, and Aldo Cibic (all trained as architects and industrial

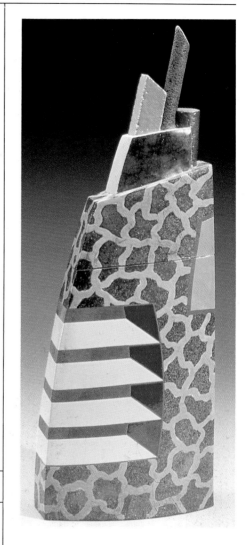

Bruce Lenore's raku "Ship," from 1984, measures 26 inches by 12 inches by 6 inches. More decorative than functional, it can be displayed most effectively on a wide shelf or perhaps atop a sideboard. It should be placed, preferably, against a solid-hued background; the contrast from this positioning picks up its oddly combined colors and forms so they can stand out to their best advantage.

Stewart Lucas' hand-painted ties sport the sort of zany patterns and color combinations of which Memphis' designers are so fond. Sottsass himself has often remarked on the similarities between the Memphis mentality in regard to furniture design and the capriciousness of the fashion business. But while Sottsass perversely stresses the fact that Memphis designs will date as surely as last year's fashions, the fact remains that both the furniture designs and clothing designs—like Lucas'—that parallel them will become collectors' items, vivid reminders of a particular place and a particular time.

designers, and who worked on a variety of projects outside Memphis under the aegis of Sottsass Associati); by fellow-travelers Branzi, de Lucchi, Martine Bedin, George James Sowden, Nathalie du Pasquier, and Gerard Taylor; as well as by several world-renowned architects, including the Japanese Arata Isozaki, the Austrian Hans Hollein, and the American Michael Graves.

The name "Memphis" itself is said to have been inspired by Bob Dylan's "Stuck Outside of Mobile with the Memphis Blues Again," a song playing on the stereo one night late in 1980, when plans for the new venture were assuming a clearer form. Later, others were to hail the name as especially appropriate, alluding as it did to both the ancient capital of Egypt and the birthplace of Elvis Presley—a juxtaposition of high and low culture that was to prove a chief characteristic of Memphis' style.

The first Memphis collection was launched in the fall of 1981, during the Milan Furniture Fair—though outside it, at the Arc '74 showroom. The forty designs—unlike those shown at, say, the biannual American furniture market at High Point, North Carolina—were not mass-produced or stocked. Many were simply prototypes, often partly handcrafted for Memphis by various manufacturers, many of whom operated in traditional crafts workshop settings rather than in techno-logical, modern-day factories.

The furniture and lamps in this first collection were striking, to say the least. Publicity, coordinated by Italian journalist Barbara Radice, was enormous. Studio Alchymia's similar work had been noticed, but its reception was muted compared to the uproar Memphis created. Reactions were far from unanimously favorable, but happily enough, the many detractors had little effect on the newborn company's efforts. Memphis already enjoyed the enthusiastic support of the manufactur-ers backing it, of those contracted to produce it, and of Italy's leading design magazines and furniture stores.

Although a number of designers are involved in Memphis, the various pieces boast a considerable degree of stylistic unity—due in part to Sottsass, who reviews proposals from sympathetic designers, and in part to what appears to be a genuine collective spirit, in which designers influence one another without too many power struggles as to whose personal vision Memphis *really* reflects. Working in this manner, the consortium has introduced two more large Memphis collections—one of sixty-four items, and one of sixty-five—since the initial *succès de scandale*. Smaller collections are expected to follow annually, while the earlier pieces will remain available. Though many were originally handcrafted or at least semihandcrafted and made to order, there is now talk of producing more Memphis pieces in larger quantities and stocking them. Indeed, large-scale production of some

George J. Sowden's "Acapulco" clock, from Memphis' 1981 collection, features the bright, clashing colors and exaggerated patterns that have become associated with the movement. Technologically, the clock is not out of the ordinary. The innovation is its functionless, beautiful decoration.

of the less intricate designs has already begun.

It might be enough to say that the Memphis designers have been inspired by sources at the margin of mainstream Western design—early twentieth-century decorative pieces; suburban Pop (and especially Milanese Pop, which perhaps has influenced Memphis' Italian members even more directly than its American equivalent); and eastern and Third World traditions—simply for the sake of creating beautiful, intriguing furniture and objects that are a pleasure to live with. But the Memphis designers see their work not only as mere objects but as political statements, existential metaphors, what you might call visible poetry, and a challenge to received notions of design—all rolled together.

NO MORE HIERARCHIES

The statement Memphis' designs make is, in part, a political one, a criticism of social hierarchies and the power structures on which those hierarchies rely. As Ettore Sottsass wrote in the *MANtransFORMS* catalog (1976) from the Cooper-Hewitt Museum in New York City, "I'd ...like it if...the more fortunate and more beautiful people, the washed and scented with their happy eyes, were companions and not masters.... if there were no more talk about the fortunate and unfortunate, of better and worse.... if instead they talked about things to do together...."

Idealistic and abstract as it may sound, this vision of a better world actually has a concrete visual equivalent in Memphis furniture. The same desire to do away with hierarchies (fortunate/unfortunate, better/worse, etc.) is reflected in Memphis' use of materials—a mix of high-class and low-class elements. The Memphis designers, crack semioticians all, are keenly aware of the cultural connotations that make a material high or low class. They know how people "read" marble as a sign of power and wealth, how they "read" plastic laminates and garish colors as signs of the supposedly tacky masses.

True to their anti-hierarchical bias, the Memphis designers scramble these connotations to the point where you cannot tell which material is high, which low. A single piece of furniture might feature a juxtaposition of materials, each bearing a contradictory cultural connotation. For example, a costly and unusual wood might be combined with chrome (high class when it was a Bauhaus trademark, but since commercialized and, therefore, low class), gaudy plastic laminate, and colored light bulbs. When combined with these low-class materials, that high-class wood may look a little cheap and certainly less classy itself; at the same time, we might come to appreciate the previously ignored beauty of those low-class materials.

Another anti-hierarchical gesture involves setting up a contradiction between material and environment. The idea of a "living room" signifies status and wealth, as does the material marble. The decorating magazines and interior designers say that this living room should be the "important" room, the showpiece, filled with furniture whose forms and materials connote status. Memphis, of course, sees things differently. To subvert the living room's accepted connotations, Memphis designers will fill it with furniture whose loud hues, ridiculous asymmetrical forms, and funky materials connote the *opposite* of status. One could say that by having a zany Memphis sideboard in your living room, you defuse the status and seriousness of that room. Furthermore, insofar as that living room is an expression of your own status, wealth, and aspirations, a Memphis sideboard might even serve to undercut your own seriousness about yourself as well.

A paradox arises here, of course: even when made out of inexpensive materials like plastic laminate, Memphis pieces cost lots of money and therefore signify a certain status. However, as Memphis widens its influence and moves toward large-scale production of at least some of its pieces, prices are beginning to come down—and with them maybe a few hierarchies, too, such as the one that distinguishes between the rich who can afford Memphis and the person with an average income who previously could not afford the handcrafted pieces.

Designer Nathalie du Pasquier alludes to the day-glo hues of the sixties, the spiky motifs seen on some 1920s Wiener Werkstaette fabrics and to African fabric patterns in the pencil case she designed in 1983 for Fiorucci. By bringing together diverse influences in a single piece, Memphis designers attempt to suggest something about the nature of our world today, where so much information is available simultaneously.

FURNITURE AS METAPHOR

These pieces carry an implicit social critique; they also confront us with new metaphors for the contemporary world. Their busy patterns, myriad colors, and combinations of unlikely elements mirror the hyperactivity, variety, and unpredictability of the Global Village in this electronic age. Even within a single piece, the elements may evoke various parts of the world (a chair's fabric may recall West African patterns, its form reminiscent of American 1940s streamline style, and its colors resembling those of Italian *sorbetti*). That same piece may bring to mind the wonder of electronics, particularly the electronics behind television, that are able to bring different parts of the world into our homes, one after the other, with just a flick of the dial. In regard to this, Memphis designer George J. Sowden is surely on the right track when he writes that "the electronic is decorative, playful, colorful," thinking, no doubt, of color television, rock video, video games, and computer graphics—media through which we, at least in part, experience our dense, chaotic world. If we accept Sowden's assumption that "the decorative [i.e., Memphis] belongs to the electronic world just as the functional belonged to the machine," we can see just how well-attuned Memphis is to the spirit of these times—and how inappropriate the calm, cool Modern designs are that it seeks to displace.

JOYFUL PESSIMISM

The excesses of Memphis' bright colors and dense patterns also bespeak a darker side of today's world. Its overwhelming, confusing, and uncontrollable superabundance is reflected in the multiplicity of colors, forms, and materials that characterize Memphis pieces. The designers responded to this dizzying, dazzling, absurd too-muchness as a cause for laughter and jubilation—a sort of more-the-merrier approach. At the same time, though, they detected something unsettling about a decadent consumer culture run amok, something depressing about an unstable world where fashions change constantly and rapidly, where all possible viewpoints are advanced simultaneously unguided by any organizing principle, and where "right" and "wrong," "true" and "false" become increasingly hard to tell apart.

Memphis designs exude both joy and nihilism. The contradictoriness of these two responses—expressed visually in the pieces themselves—lends them their special poignance. Not surprisingly, Sottsass and company are well aware of these contradictions. Sottsass remarked, "if a society plans obsolescence, the only possible enduring design is one that deals with that obsolescence, a design that comes to terms with it, maybe accelerating it, maybe confronting it, maybe ironizing it, maybe getting along with it.... And then I don't understand why enduring design is better than disappearing design...."

In this acceptance of transience—an attitude directly opposed to that of the Modernist designers and architects who believed that they had developed a style whose permanent validity was inarguable—Sottsass reveals his allegiance to Eastern philosophy. Some might call that

This brightly striped fabric from Missoni gives an idea of how Italy's more conservative designers are taking some of Memphis' color schemes and modifying them so that they may become palatable to a broader audience. The colors here are less peculiar but equally playful. The fabric can be sensational on just a few throw pillows or as upholstery for a big, shapeless sofa whose form is not meant to be played up in the first place.

acceptance pessimistic, even fatalistic. And yet rather than establish rules to counteract obsolescence and time's inevitable passage, Memphis designs accept this passage with high-spirited humor. In this respect, the pieces might be seen as the physical equivalents of koans: those absurd questions Zen masters pose to their students, which have no real answers but rather are intended to help the mind leap over preconceptions. Memphis, unlike Modernism, does not offer a rational, utopian answer to solve the world's woes. Indeed, Memphis accepts that the world is a pretty woeful place—and a pretty funny one.

FURNITURE AS POEM

Memphis' poetic and spiritual aspects are harder to define. Sottsass holds a fascination with the ancient Egyptian, Sumerian, Central American, and Jewish cultures that have "left traces in our memories, from magic to religion to fanaticism [and] technologies of life which are not always rational..." This outlook would certainly seem to be expressed in Memphis' irrational-looking designs. And something about those designs calls not so much for reasoned argumentation but for reverie, for a reflectiveness as drifting and unpredictable as the designs themselves. They give rise to fantasies—indeed, they seem to have emerged from fantasies and hypnagogic visions. For all that they partake of the spirit of today's world, they also encourage an inwardness that does not embrace today's upwardly mobile motion. Designer Emilio Ambasz noted that, for him, "Memphis' fascination resides in the fact that, having realized the designer has little chance of affecting physically the larger urban environment, he has chosen to take refuge in the interior of the house—the last domain of individual freedom."

Matteo Thun's ceramic pieces, designed in 1981 for Memphis, can lend a whimsical quality to table settings. These vases make handsome centerpieces for a table. What's more, though their shapes are weird enough (recalling the Tin Woodsman), the colors are not as strident as some Memphis colors; they may strike consumers as better hues for blending in with more conservative interiors.

Marco Zanini's "Alpha Centauri" flower vase from Memphis' 1982 collection has a quality that, appropriately for its name, calls science fiction to mind. Made in clear, blue, green, red, and aquamarine glass, the vase is crafted according to time-honored modes of glassmaking. Only its form is revolutionary—another instance of a Memphis designer bringing together two contradictions in a single piece.

Memphis takes refuge in the interior of the house *and* in the mind's interior, the imagination. With that in mind, I have attempted to offer (I am tempted to say "risked") both a rational and an imaginative response to the designs. Once people get through the poetic, spiritual, metaphorical, and political aspects of Memphis, they often ask: "What do I do with this stuff?" Answers to such a question will be given in due course. But a Memphis design is a poetic object, akin to the surrealist object as defined by André Breton: "nothing less than the objectification of the very act of dreaming, its transformation into reality." Given this definition, and given the thinking that in part underlies Memphis' poetic irrationality, I trust the reader will forgive my occasional indulgence in some dreaming of my own—a dreaming set off by the Memphis pieces, and one that I hope will seem as illogical, subjective, open-ended, and playful as those pieces. In presenting these "dream sequences," I hope to suggest possible ways of responding to and enjoying Memphis that are just as important as both the ways in which its designs can actually be put to use and the critique these pieces offer of today's world.

IT'S POETRY, BUT DOES IT WORK?

Memphis designer Marco Zanini has stated that Memphis "is more intellectual than commercial." The speculations offered above—only the tip of the Memphis iceberg, given all the rhetoric that swirls around this furniture in Italy and abroad—would seem to suggest as much. The accompanying illustrations may convey what could be viewed as the impracticality of Memphis designs, which could in turn discourage potential buyers. But too much has been made of the impracticality of Memphis pieces. Although there are exceptions, most of them are functional and comfortable. Their odd look, however, causes us to revise our notions of comfort and function—or to adopt new ones.

"Function is the final possibility of connection between an object and life," Ettore Sottsass declares. With this in mind we may be obliged to change our lives somewhat in accordance with the pieces. This is not as outrageous as it sounds, for Memphis' designs are never intentionally or cruelly inconvenient, nor gratuitously contrary to our expectations of what furniture should be. Rather, they ask us to look more closely at how we live in rooms and how we interact with the objects in them. For instance, just as sexual fantasies and dreaming answer our need for wish-fulfillment that the waking world cannot always provide, some of the Memphis lamps may answer not our need for practical lighting but a psychological need for a glow with something magical and inexplicable about it. Thus, some Memphis lamps more closely resemble dreamlike cult objects than strictly functional sources of illumination.

Then there are storage pieces, which look as if they could hold about a third as much as a far less expensive piece of equal size bought at your local unpainted-furniture shop. Yet these pieces encourage us to examine our attitudes toward possessions—to ask ourselves why we own as much as we do; whether we really need all that we have; and whether we need to store it all in the orderly manner dictated by mass-produced storage pieces. While traditional crisp angles and straight lines may look like the "best" design solution, they were chosen because they "make sense" and because they are the most cost-effective way to manufacture such a piece.

This aspect of Memphis that challenges us to question the way we live is perhaps the most important of all. We like to think that in this very unstable world, some things will never change; lamps, tables, chairs—objects that we associate with our earliest memories of home are among these. But the Memphis designers want to cure us of our nostalgic yearnings for that perfect little world we so often wish to go back to when confronted with the "messy vitality" outside. Since we cannot travel backward in time, such yearnings are impossible to fulfill. In offering us their furniture to live with, they are giving us a chance to live lives of our own, made up as we go along, not rooted in childhood. The challenge is not an easy one to meet. With some of the more awkward and uncomfortable pieces, it is unmeetable. But as Sottsass admits, "Memphis furniture is very intense, and . . . it can only live with very intense people, with highly evolved and self-sufficient people. Self-sufficient because I am thinking of evolved people as people who know how to run their lives properly in society without having themselves protected by any institution, even a cultural one. It is up to each one of us to decide whether we are intense enough to undertake the reevaluations Memphis demands."

MEMPHIS MARCHES ON

Many people have accused Memphis, despite its intellectual heftiness, of being mere surface flash, hype, something for the trendies, a novelty that will go out of fashion within the next few years. Sottsass himself seemed to encourage this view: he declared that in five years' time Memphis will be dead or else transformed into something else. In sync as he is with the novelty-crazed zeitgeist, however, such predictions strengthen his position rather than weaken it. "We are not designing for eternity," he stated. "For me obsolescence is just the sugar of life." Whether or not Memphis itself is a passing fad, this brief introduction should suggest that it is extremely interesting in its own right.

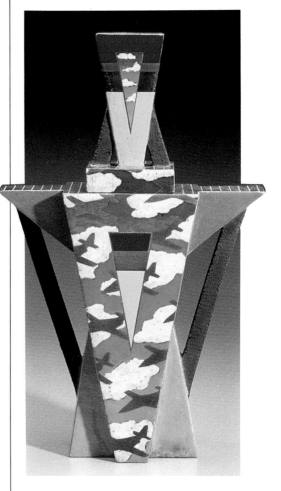

American craftsperson Bruce Lenore designed this raku piece, called "Ace," which looks like a robotoid figure whose chest reflects a sky filled with cumulus clouds and jet bombers. Although it sports a toylike quality, you will most likely not forget that "Ace" is considerably more expensive than most toys. And yet, as childlike as it seems, in years to come, it may prove to be a wise investment. Lenore's sense of color and pattern mark him as an inventor very much in the Memphis mode.

In fact, for all the doubting Thomases and Ettores, there are many others who feel that Memphis is here to stay. Already in the United States, Europe, and Japan, a great deal of furniture, furnishings, and clothing are clearly Memphis-inspired; some from established designers who, under the Memphis spell, have changed direction in mid-career, others from young or student designers who take to the style like the proverbial ducks to water. Some of these designs are not accurate imitations as much as wonderfully imaginative parallels to the Memphis pieces. Some are handcrafted, others mass-produced. Even a number of the more derivative pieces are amusing and visually pleasing. As with many design groups, some of the ensuing objects are well-executed, while others are admittedly feeble, opportunistic rip-offs.

Whether good or bad, though, all of these designs suggest that Memphis is by no means slated for extinction but very much alive. In some cases displays of the colorful Memphis-inspired pieces are merely being used to lure customers into stores, the displayers not believing that his customers will really buy them. In other cases, though, people *are* buying, and, as the American home-furnishings industry believes, consumers will buy more of it in the forseeable future. "Memphis is kitsch—the Cyndi Lauper of design," quips Soovia Janis' national sales manager Henry Wallengren. "We can't ignore Memphis anymore," counters a buyer from a Federated Department Stores unit, "It's just not going away." But perhaps designer Alessandro Mendini has offered the most eloquent prediction when he states: "By now it's only a question of time—the image of Italian furniture will change beyond recognition. A new attitude will replace the style that has lasted many years, and the fixed points on which today's furniture rests will vanish along with its philosophy. The experiments, exhibitions, intuitions, and prototypes [of Memphis] are explicitly launching the 'New International Style'—the forthcoming neo-modern design." World leader in design that Italy is, it is safe to assume that what changes there will change everywhere else, too.

ELITIST?

Ever since the Arts and Crafts movement, countless designers have sought to create quality design that is affordable to the masses. Often this proved impossible, for production costs would put their designs

This austere yet at the same time hyperkinetic interior boasts a rug designed by Ettore Sottsass, with a pattern that recalls—perhaps intentionally—the modern-day hieroglyphs devised by New York artist Keith Haring.

out of most people's reach. However, by exploiting industrial technology in the interests of both economic feasibility and physical comfort, Modern designers did succeed in creating "good design" for the masses—very much to their credit.

Memphis, on the other hand, begins by questioning the very *idea* of production for the masses. Today, anyone with any business sense knows that you just cannot make something—whether a new kind of chocolate, a stereo, or a sofa—and hope to get rich on it unless it can be sold to a lot of people. Common sense tells you that the less money it costs to make chocolate bars, stereos, or sofas, the higher that item's markup can be. Profits become even more assured when you know that there is a definite market for a given commodity. And so the savvy manufacturer asks: Will people buy what I'm selling?

Memphis seeks to escape this vicious cycle in which the mass market determines the design. Its designers have grown sick of too many sofas designed to meet what are said to be popular demands, which they see as stifling to their individuality and creativity. And it does not seem too farfetched to claim that a great many interesting, provocative and beautiful sofas, lamps, plays, novels, and paintings will never become commercially available at all, since they lack mass appeal. Memphis tries to circumvent this situation. Its pieces—particularly the earlier ones—are defiantly *un*marketable. Their forms are bizarre, despite the fact that everyone agrees that "bizarre" won't sell. Their production costs are high, so forget big sales. As for whether Memphis makes money, that fact is best known to its accountants. My guess is that it is perhaps breaking even, and that, at least initially, profit was not the point (one reason why the company has had to be "backed" by financially more successful ones, as well as by the for-money work of several of its designers).

Memphis' high prices lead people to accuse it of being elitist. Underlying that accusation is the assumption that, today, only a product with mass appeal—and because of that appeal, a reasonable price—is valid and praiseworthy. Now Memphis, with an eye on profit like everyone else, is moving toward mass production, which will probably not be determined so much by "marketability" as by what the designers feel like creating.

American architect and designer Vincas Meilus designed this colorful table, one that recalls earlier American pieces—particularly mass-produced "Moderne" metal porch furniture of the thirties and forties. His design works in much the same way that Memphis' pieces do, with their allusions to colors, patterns, and types of everyday furnishings passersby can see in many of today's Italian suburbs.

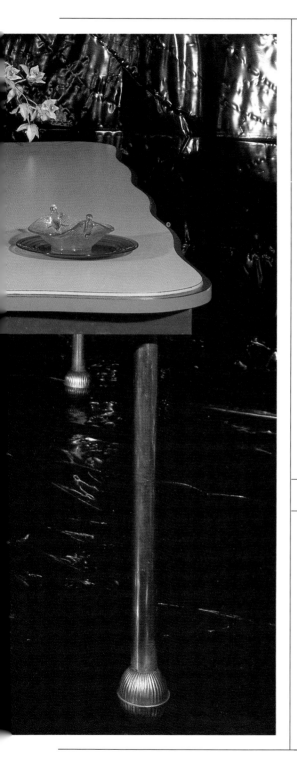

Of course this uncompromising self-indulgence attitude *is* elitist. It assumes that the designer knows better than the marketing, sales, and production people—and the consumer—what the best design is. In this way, Memphis does seem to reinstate one hierarchy that democracy and mass culture would do away with: that which assumes the artist is somehow more enlightened or insightful than the masses. Ettore Sottsass, however, has written movingly of how wonderful it would be if even *that* distinction—of artist versus non-artist—disappeared, if we lived in a world where we *all* created beautiful, imaginative, exalting things.

Suffice to say, Memphis' so-called elitism is a protest against the demands of mass culture and the stifling effect of those demands on the individual—a remarkably successful protest it is. Such protests are usually labeled "avant-garde," "fringe," and when not dismissed, must struggle for recognition and funding, rarely achieving financial success. Or they must compromise to some extent with mass taste. But Memphis, as has been noted by several critics, is the world's most popular avant-garde movement. You might even call it elitism for the masses, though if it actually does become that, Memphis would no longer be what it started out to be. Its original intent—the criticism of the constraints mass culture puts on the individual's intellect and creativity—will have been lost. The Memphis "look," on the other hand, will remain, as is abundantly evident from the way affordable, *none*litist Memphis-like designs have started entering the market. Given the strangeness of that look (let alone the revolutionary thinking behind it), that is a stupendous accomplishment in and of itself.

ABOUT THIS BOOK

This book will examine both a sampling of the nearly two hundred Memphis pieces currently available as well as those inspired variations on their highly original themes. Short individual chapters are devoted to lamps; tables; chairs; sofas; storage; ceramics, silver, and glassware; electronics; patterns; interiors in which the pieces have been used effectively; and, finally, wearables. Anyone coming upon Memphis for the first time is likely to be confused as to what the designs *are*, how to respond to them, and how to use them. With this in mind, each chapter includes some abstract reflections as well as straightforward suggestions for placing the various pieces in one's home. A source list, included at the end, gives names and addresses of shops and showrooms where the Memphis originals and the Memphis-inspired pieces can be bought.

chapter 1

Since the 1960s, Italian designers have made a specialty of lamps and lighting fixtures whose forms have epitomized Modern sleekness. Their tungsten-halogen or quartz bulbs—the kind previously used only in industrial settings—have brought a new, cool, clear, and energy-efficient illumination into the home. Those lamps meant to provide ambient lighting were handsome and cleanlined. Others, intended to illuminate tasks, were marvels of flexibility and function. Whether designed for task or ambient lighting, these lamps lacked ornamentation. Various metals were the favored materials. Color was limited to black, white, or the tone of whichever metal had been employed in the design (aluminum, chrome, or brass), with a bright primary hue included as an accent occasionally. Many of these fixtures are still available, as are the American knockoffs they inspired. Several of the originals have become contemporary classics, including those manufactured by Artemide, the Italian company that represents Memphis in the United States. Ernesto Gismondi, its founder and chairman, was one of the key people responsible for getting Memphis off the ground as a financially viable operation.

Needless to say, Memphis has veered away from this steep and monochromatic path; its lamps are colorful and toylike. Some (particularly the more recent designs) are structurally more like a typical Modern desk lamp or torchere, with a base, a stem, and a bulb encased in a reflector. Others might have a tall, slim stem with bulb and reflector perched on top of it. Others still are organized far more whimsically, often providing little task illumination; nor do they resemble the lamps with which we are most familiar. Usually there is no orthodox base or shade. The bulb of these whimsical renditions is often bare, encased in a little metal box or perched atop a narrow stem containing the necessary wiring. The base, on the other hand, comprises the main body of the object and looks more like a curious sculpture that just happens to have a bulb on it than a lamp. Indeed, Memphis lamps *are* luminous sculptures of bizarre form, appealing in and of themselves, quite apart from any function they might serve. Their materials—especially wood finished in plastic laminate and metal, as well as aluminum, ceramic, and Plexiglas—are also unusual, strangely colored, and combined in odd, gratuitous ways.

I do not use the word *gratuitous* pejoratively. Memphis lamps are *pleasingly* gratuitous and, like the Mad Hatter, amiably batty. In this, they contradict and enlarge on our very notion of what a lamp might be.

In life as we know it, we turn on a lamp for a reason: to read, to cook, to go over our bank balances, to see each other, to get a better look at our cats' whiskers. The irrationality of a Memphis lamp distracts us from these rational activities. Looking at one—odd, dreamlike object that it is—may plunge us into daydreams of our own, where we can imagine other lands, other planets, other centuries, other levels of existence where such a lamp would fit in very nicely. We lose ourselves in reverie for the sheer pleasure of it.

Memphis designer Matteo Thun's "Santa Monica" hanging lamp, offered in the 1983 collection, has a simple white porcelain shade. Its eccentric shape and its practicality make it an ideal piece for those interested in Memphis' wit yet disconcerted by the uselessness of some of its designs. This lamp is produced in rather large quantities and so is priced more reasonably than most other Memphis pieces.

LAMPS

Memphis' 1981 collection included Martine Bedin's little "Super" lamp (left), which looks a bit like an electric porcupine. This lamp will not provide much light; however, in a sparsely furnished room with lots of floor space, it might be kept on the floor as a design objet. The spare backgrounds of this Dallas bedroom (right) allow George James Sowden's bed and Michele de Lucchi's lamp—both from Memphis—to take center stage. If one wishes to "do" an entire room in Memphis pieces, it is sometimes a good idea to keep the backgrounds pristine, since the pieces themselves make such a strong impression. For those who prefer a less single-minded approach, a few Memphis pieces might be mixed in with furniture or objects in other styles.

Turn on an "Ashoka" lamp and on goes the lamp, shedding not very much in the way of usable light, but just an ambient glow from a Space Age menorah. Your imagination takes hold and thanks to your own imaginative flights, your humdrum life may become transformed, if not into the Eldorado we all long for, then at least into a world away from routine, that is a bit different, tinged with an unexpected and pleasing hue and, if only in a small way, enlarged.

The first Memphis lamps (of which "Ashoka" was one) were perhaps more suited to dreamy contemplation than daily use. After all, upon first seeing "Ashoka," you might not know quite *what* to do with it. Put it on an end table? A mantelpiece? Atop an étagère? On the floor?

But with Memphis' resounding success, some designers are now thinking of pieces (including lamps) with lower price tags and

greater practicality. Matteo Thun's reasonably priced and best-selling "Santa Monica" hanging lamp, for instance, is clearly meant to be suspended above a dining table and to light up the tabletop and the area around it. Yet it too has its mysterious side. Its ceramic shade recalls the metal covers of recessed ceiling fans in New York City subway cars, whose shapes in turn recall streamlined Moderne lighting fixtures—fixtures that might well be found in some streamlined planetarium in a more laid-back version of Fritz Lang's *Metropolis.* Its shade functions as and is a lamp shade. But might it not also be a model of the planets' orbits, with the large spherical bulb in its center the sun? Put it over your dining table, and it will light up your card game or midnight snack. But, like the celestial diagrams Joseph Cornell often included in his constructions, it will also, in some magical way, link

your room to far-off places, will evoke long journeys across silent tracts of space, sunlight falling through a window of a room on another, uninhabited planet...

Granted, then, that some of the Memphis lamps are useful primarily as poetic objects. Others, despite their evocative quality, seem more down-to-earth. But will a Memphis lamp fit in with the furniture you already own? The answer would, I think, be Yes. In fact, for anyone interested in Memphis in an enthusiastic but limited way, a lamp would be a sensible acquisition no matter how a home is furnished. All of these lamps are imaginatively designed; and those created by any of the Memphis designers have a similar feel to them. Such lamps and light fixtures are striking enough visually to hold their own in *any* setting. A lamp, then, can be effective in a room filled with anything from overstuffed, chintz-covered sofas

Sottsass Associati, headed by Ettore Sottsass and composed of the "core" designers of Memphis, created the brilliant interiors for Grace Designs' showroom in Houston (left). The designers kept a basic color palette and played around instead with the room's architecture.

Lampes Drimmer, a French manufacturer, commissioned several of Memphis' young designers to create a lamp collection for them. The "Memphis" collection—not to be confused with Memphis itself—includes this lamp (above) by Nathalie du Pasquier. It boasts an earthenware base and the lively patterns with which this designer first made a name for herself. The "Memphis" collection is available through George Kovacs Lighting.

to minimalist built-ins to so-called "lifestyle" furniture or hand-me-downs. Of course, the lamp itself will be jarring, and evocative and funny. But because it is relatively small, it will not dominate the room. Rather, it will make its statement, and otherwise keep to itself. Still, you will not forget that it is there. Nor will you want to.

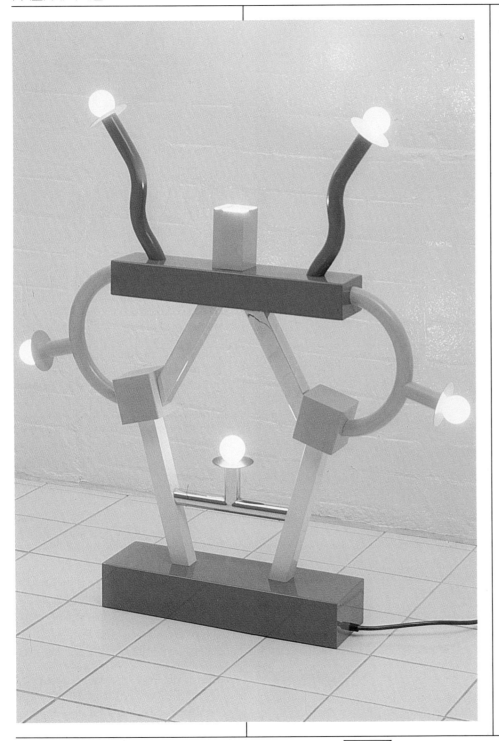

It is difficult to tell from the picture (above) just how large-scaled Michele de Lucchi's "Oceanic" lamp is. In person, it almost resembles an undersized sea serpent. One little black-and-white painted metal candy cane on this table lamp's pink base contains the on-off switch, the other its cord. The metal-encased bulb, provides more than adequate light to read by.

Ettore Sottsass' "Ashoka" lamp, (left), for the first—1981—Memphis collection, is of painted metal. The little round bulbs at the ends of the lamp's various tendrils seem almost vulnerable, as if they would recoil when touched. "Ashoka" is one of Memphis' most expensive lamps.

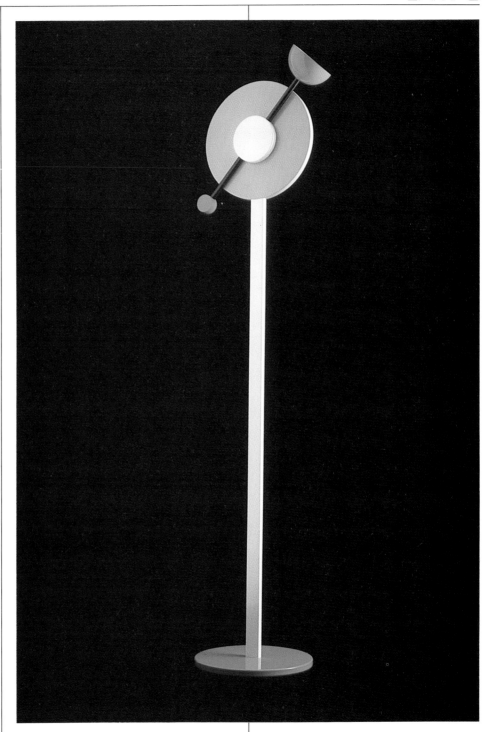

Designer Martine Bedin's floor lamp, "Charleston," is part of Memphis' 1984 collection. It is made of painted aluminum and has a halogen bulb. The lamp looks *toylike* enough to make it echt Memphis. Yet its swiveling arm, ending in a blue cup that contains the light bulb, is not unlike the sort of feature a less quirky-looking Italian floor lamp might have—one that allows you to alter the direction of the light shed with a mere flick of the hand. This feature is more practical than some that grace other Memphis lamps. But it shows how, without sacrificing whimsy, a Memphis piece can do what more conventional designs do.

The chair is the design object par excellence of twentieth-century design. Despite their stylistic differences, Mackintosh, Hoffmann, Breuer, Aalto, Le Corbusier, Mies van der Rohe, Rietveld, Saarinen, Eames, Wegner, and Jacobsen have all made their most memorable design statements with the chairs they created. The challenge of designing the Perfect Chair—one that is comfortable, practical, handsome, capable (thanks to industrial technology) of being mass-produced and, if possible, affordable to large numbers of people—has proved most enticing to Modern designers. For the most part, these designers have met the challenge successfully, a fact that accounts for the enduring popularity of their chairs and for the classic status conferred upon so many of them.

Would-be disrupter of the Modern tradition that it is, Memphis might have tried to supersede these twentieth-century classics with iconoclastic but equally inviting chairs of its own. But as any designer will freely admit, designing a good chair isn't easy. Some of this century's best chairs reached their final form only after extensive experimentation with new technology. Memphis, with its emphasis on handcrafting, would appear uninterested in such possibilities, and its designs, with their air of quick improvisation and unlimited free-

dom, run counter to the notion of slow, patient development.

And so it is not surprising that Memphis chairs, inventive as they are, cannot compete with this century's great designs. Memphis' lightweight, more structural chairs particularly are uncomfortable, which immediately puts them at a disadvantage in the American market, at least, where comfort is considered important in whether a chair will sell. Nevertheless, with several of these chairs, Memphis is moving into mass production. Their prices, therefore, are much lower than those of most other Mem-

CHAIRS

phis pieces, and these whimsical designs are sure to enjoy greater popularity, although it is doubtful that they will wholly replace the more comfortable, more predictable, and, to our eyes, more boring Breuer chair. They work best as occasional chairs; as the only chairs in someone's home, they would perhaps be unfortunate choices.

Memphis' upholstered chairs are more successful, carrying on in the tradition of upholstered chairs by such designers as Josef Hoffman and Jean Michel Frank,

and—though Memphis designers may be loath to admit it—those by well-known Italian contemporaries such as Mario Bellini and Vico Magistretti. These large-scaled but light-hearted pieces *are* quite comfortable, and their pleasing bold colors, patterns, and forms have already had a noticeable effect on chairs by Italian designers outside the Memphis fold—designers against whose work Memphis was rebelling in the first place. These designers, however, still manage to concern themselves with both ergonomics and industrial techniques, even as their attitude toward decora-

Marco Zanini's "Lucrezia" chair, included in Memphis' 1984 collection, has an aluminum frame. It is interesting to note how unindustrial this metal looks here. The chair is upholstered with an opulent cotton fabric, designed by Ettore Sottsass, that enhances the feeling of richness and elegance. Zanini achieved this depth of feeling merely by including several sensual curves in what is basically a simple, straightforward design.

chapter 2

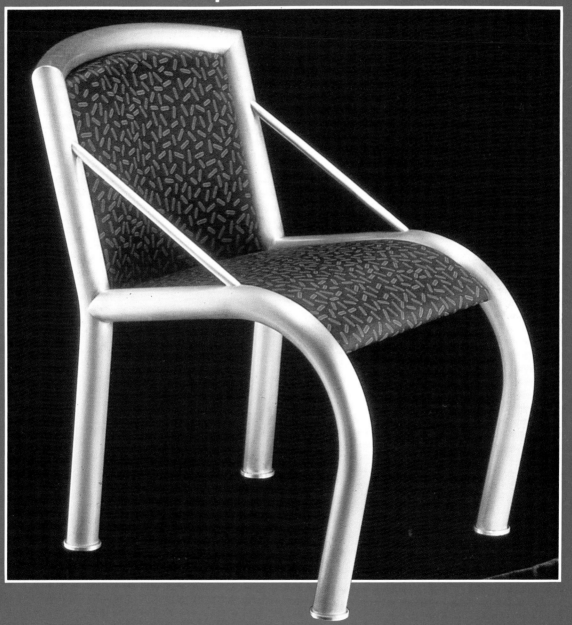

In an effort to reach a broader market, Memphis now offers chairs that, while still as unpredictable as earlier pieces, are inexpensive and produced in larger quantities. Of these, Michele de Lucchi's "First" (above) and George J. Sowden's "Palace" (opposite) are best-sellers. Architect Robert Venturi's collection of chairs for Knoll, which includes "Art Deco" (right), consists of cartoonish pieces whose lighthearted spirit recalls some Memphis pieces. The pattern shown is silk-screened.

tion loosens up. Memphis, on the other hand, concentrates almost exclusively on the chair's appearance.

Functioning chairs, then, for the most part constitute Memphis' less brilliant efforts. Given Memphis' intellectual bent, however, its chairs carry a multiplicity of symbolic connotations. Indeed, Ettore Sottsass' essay "The Chair" in the Cooper-Hewitt Museum's *MANtransFORMS* catalog (1976) shows just how much thought has gone into this particular piece of furniture's sociological, mystical, psychological, and political significance. In the essay, Sottsass voices his distrust of the chair as a symbol of power. He wonders, too, at how the chair provides a metaphorical means for us to sit on the world (as represented by a chair's seat), thereby controlling it and also defacing it (with our behinds). And then he asks, why do we prefer to do so many things sitting rather than standing? Further speculations follow, all of them fascinating.

In fact, Sottsass and several other Memphis designers have created chairs whose symbolic complexity equals the complexity of those speculations. While not always comfortable, the chairs are often thought-provoking. People may argue that a chair should be comfortable *before* it is thought-provoking, but Memphis is not necessarily interested in making life comfortable. Rather, it would have us question life as

The chairs in this model interior designed by Ettore Sottsass have a strange, anthropomorphic quality about them. It is anyone's guess which of the chairs will try to ascend the patterned staircase first, though all of them look capable of doing so. The furniture here is actually less idiosyncratic than the room's plan, with its seemingly purposeless but intriguing "grand stairway."

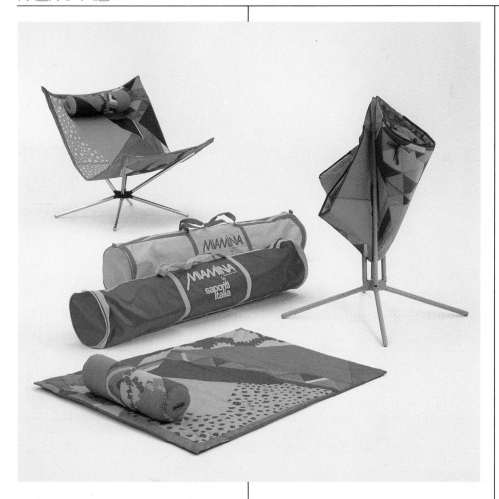

The Memphis influence on other Italian designers today is unmistakable. Designer Salvati Tresoldi's "Miamina" chair (left), with its splashy colors and vivid pattern, shares a similarly lighthearted sensibility. This chair's more practical aspects, however—the fact that it is foldable, for instance—suggest that functionality, the strong point of Modern design, need not be sacrificed for the sake of decorativeness.

American architect Robert Venturi's furniture collection for Knoll International includes this cartoonlike reinterpretation of a Chippendale chair (right). True to his aesthetic of complexity and contradiction, Venturi here combines aspects of many design themes: Alvar Aalto's furniture designs, traditional English chair design, and—in his use of a colorful plastic laminate to cover the chair—Memphis design.

we know it—and to do so without any certainty that our questions will be answered. Indeed, to sit on a Memphis chair is to sit on a question mark. Sitting and being comfortable are the least of it. These chairs make us question what we are doing even as we sit in them. Like successful psychotherapy, they demand that we be conscious of all that we are doing.

As an example of just *how* a chair might do this, take Peter Shire's regal yet ridiculous "Bel Air." With its cartoon hues and goofy excrescences, this jester's throne (which also happens to be one of Memphis' more comfortable chairs) mocks the very idea of power. Sitting in that chair, you may ask yourself (à la David Byrne), "How did I get here?" At this point in time you'd see everyone sitting around talking, having formed a little tribe, each one taking seriously what he or she says and does (since that is part of the sitting-around-and-talking ritual)—and to go on talking while you're sitting on this ludicrous chair is like talking with a shoe on your head or dressing in cap and bells. Who would dare say that the little tribal gathering, that sitting here in a ritualistic group this way—even the *very notion of rituals*—has something silly and fragile and deluding about it? "Well why are we sitting here anyway?" "What else could we be doing?" "What is there *to do*?" "Nothing to be done," says

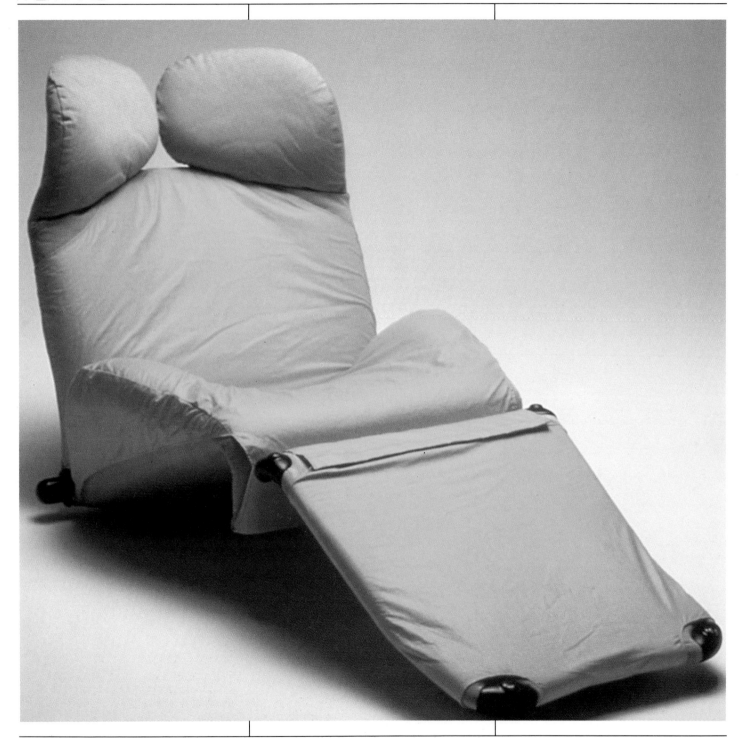

Samuel Beckett. With the next question, an infinite series of questions follow, the sense of hilariousness mounts, and power diminishes: the power words have of answering our most profound questions; the power money gives us; the power we try to have over each other; the power social rituals have of making us do things in prescribed ways; the power relationships have of binding people to each other; the power a room has to make us order our lives in a particular way; the power this sentence has of telling you something (as if it were not within you to find out everything there is to find out, about Memphis and anything else, for yourself). All this because of the hilarious presence of that "Bel Air" chair.

And then you might ask, "What have we got without power?" Not despair, Memphis says, but questions, questions, still more questions, and infinite interpretations—and no more illusions. This is what makes Memphis' chairs hard not only on the back but on the mind as well.

Michael Braun's "Arc" chair (above), of lacquered steel with canvas stretched over its seat, back, and arms, is available through Dennis Miller Associates, as are the E. B. Jackson rug, Bruce Keiser table, and Daniel Lansner screen.

Japanese designer Toshiyuki Kita's "Wink" chair (opposite) boasts "ears" like Mickey Mouse's on its back. It is a perfect example of how the whimsy associated with Memphis design can be translated into furniture that, while somewhat less playful than the Italian originals, has an air of comfort about it wholly missing in many of the Memphis pieces.

47

Accustomed as we are to furniture whose colors blend in with a room's backgrounds, we may wonder what to do with this gaudy, Memphis-like chair by Milo Baughman (above). Does it belong in a room as colorful as it is? Not necessarily. Memphis values unevenness over smoothness, and so would deem it correct for a chair like this one to stick out like the proverbial sore thumb in an otherwise neutral-toned interior.

A pair of George J. Sowden's "Palace" armchairs (right), in lacquered wood, regard each other across the expanse of a glass-topped table in the furniture showroom Sottsass Associati designed for Grace Designs in Houston. Admittedly severe in its form, the "Palace" chair boasts brightly colored legs, arms, and top, which lend a humorous edge to the piece.

Martine Bedin's "Regent" armchair, from Memphis' 1983 collection, is made of metal, briar and lacquered wood. It is one of Memphis' more inexpensive chairs and marks an attempt on the part of its designer to offer a saleable piece of furniture whose saleability does not necessitate a sacrifice of the freewheeling inventiveness that typifies earlier Memphis pieces. This chair's bent metal legs recall the bent chrome tubing of forties kitchen furniture.

chapter 3

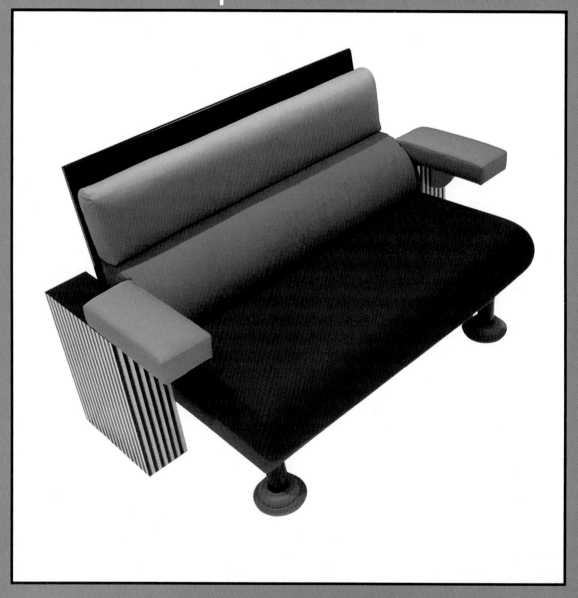

Nothing in a living room proves so inviting as the sight of a big, cushy sofa. You might imagine a different world, where life itself would be so pleasantly padded that you wouldn't need a particular piece of furniture to sink down into: life itself would be as comfortable as snuggling into a capacious old couch.

Memphis sofas and chaise lounges would seem only to indicate their designers' hopes that the world will someday become so cozy. For they offer no refuge from the real world but oblige us to maintain our alert, out-in-the-world stance even while we are at home. Memphis sofas are not the big, soft, protecting ones for shifting positions, flopping around, slouching, putting our legs up, and doing all the other things everyone likes to do on sofas. Hard-edged—almost unyieldingly so—they discourage such behavior. Rather, they seem best suited to people who do not like to sit down and relax for too long—busy, active types always on the go.

This hard-edged effect constitutes the flip side of a design philosophy that would draw the outer world's complexities and contradictions into the home's once-calm inner sanctum. Memphis would have us stay in that inner sanctum for as short a time as possible; it proposes "talking" designs, ones that communicate cultural meanings. Yet, paradoxically—and this may be one of the shortcomings of these designs—they can get so yaketty that they forget to provide congenial settings for our own communications with one another.

Visually, however, these sofas and chaises are delightful. At least in America, the sofa is often thought of as a "grown-up" piece of furniture, the kind you acquire only when you have a "real" place of your own. Yet Memphis sofas are disarmingly silly and childlike—overgrown, futuristic playthings or shrunken, toylike minimonuments. Like so many of the Memphis pieces, their colors and patterns are vibrant (though recent designs feature more subtle hues), their materials surprising (ranging from marble and cotton chintz to metal and plastic laminate), and their forms imaginative.

In terms of their functions and implications, however, these pieces may be somewhat less than amiable. Unlike most sofas and chaise lounges, the Memphis pieces address themselves not primarily to our backs and buttocks but to our minds. They are not "about" physical comfort, but they comment on what it means in our society to sit on a sofa or recline on a chaise. The Memphis designers, ornery as poltergeists, would rob us of our middle-class comforts: our genial evenings at home complacently talking, watching our televisions or VCRs, or listening to our stereos. Indeed, these pieces of furniture might be taken as a series of jokes about and critiques of the very idea of sitting down and participating in such activities (see Chapter Three for jokes and critiques that are carried to extremes by Memphis chairs). No doubt bourgeois ideology would have us sit and relax only in certain places and have us work only in certain others, rigidly separat-

Michele de Lucchi's "Lido" sofa is made of printed plastic laminate, lacquered wood, and metal, and upholstered with woolen fabric. From Memphis, it of course looks futuristic, but not dauntingly so, recalling as it does colorful childhood toys. One could see it working well in rooms furnished with pieces in earlier futuristic styles like Art Deco or 1940s moderne, or even the blocky, densely ornamented 1920s Wiener Werkstaette designs.

SOFAS

Andrea Branzi, who designed this "Century" dormeuse, is one of Memphis' most intellectual designers. The piece is almost atypical for Memphis, with its rigid lines and sober colors. Clearly, though, the piece is for show. It does not look at all inviting, though its sleek lines and carefully balanced planes of color lend it an impressively sculptural quality.

ing labor and leisure in the interests of capital. The German critic Theodor Adorno argued that Schönberg's music was meant to make our minds work and not reward us with the supposedly infantile pleasures suited to capitalist leisure time; in much the same way, Memphis sofas make us question the nature of relaxing at home rather than actually letting us relax.

And yet I, for one, wonder if this furniture opposes the status quo as effectively as its designers might think. "You *can't* sit down and relax here!" screech these garish, wildly patterned objects. Yet we must not forget one of their inspirations is the commercial Pop designs of suburbia's shrill-hued fast-food chains. They are amusingly tasteless not only for naive aesthetic reasons but

for heartily capitalistic ones, too. Their designers know exactly what they were doing with those bright colors, keeping people moving in and out, in the interest of quick turnover. Memphis may take a more ironic attitude toward such crassly manipulative design, but the effect of its own designs may not be all that different from the effect of the ones it is parodying.

For those seduced by Memphis' visual allure but put off by what it lacks in physical comfort, American elaborators on Memphis themes have retained some of the visual pizzazz of these sofas while providing comfort, too. In doing so, they produce furniture that may upset the status quo, while still appealing to more people than the stern if stimulating originals.

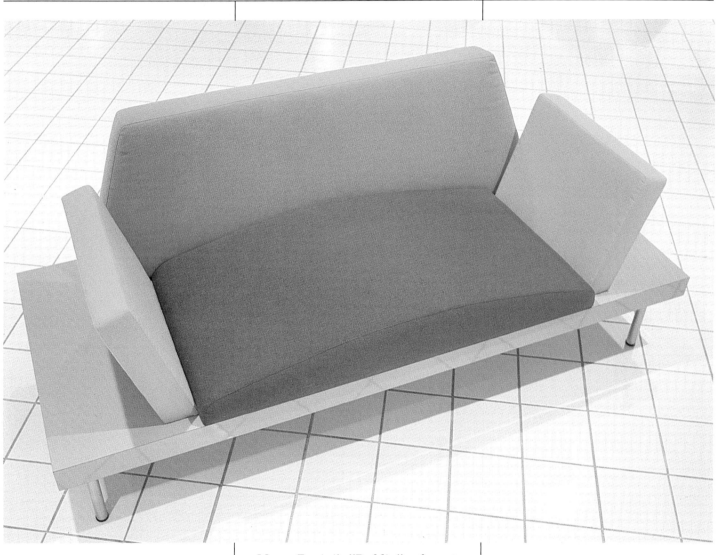

Marco Zanini's "Dublin" sofa seats
two, is structured of wood and
plastic laminate, and has four
splayed metal legs that recall the
"best" of motel lobby furniture.
Indeed, the piece has an antiseptic
air to it—intentional, of course—that
parodies the stamped-out furniture
designs one sees in fast-food chains.
The colors, too, recall the bright,
efficient interiors of many such
eateries.

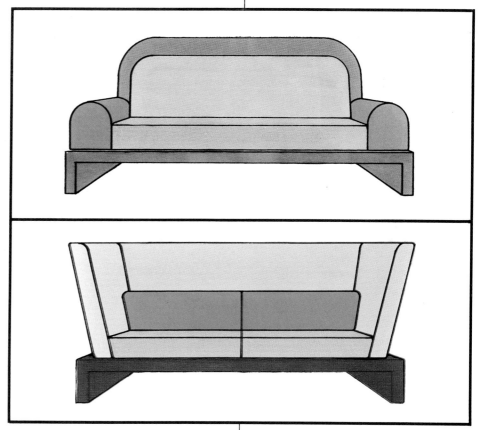

Memphis designer Matteo Thun (left) is shown here with a sofa he designed for a German manufacturer. Its voluptuous contours recall the sort of pieces you love to sink into and doze off on. But the violent juxtaposition of shapes that, by ordinary standards, just do not go together shakes us up. This is exactly what Memphis wants to do: to shake us awake and remind us of just how uncomfortable our world really is. To add to this paradox (that appears often in Memphis designs), Thun has made a sofa that, though it looks very uncomfortable, is actually a pleasure to sit on.

Milo Baughman is one of America's most adventurous designers working for a large furniture company. He was inspired by Memphis when he set about designing these colorful sofas (above), sketches of which are shown here. The American furniture industry is notoriously conservative, so it is to Baughman's credit—and to the credit of Thayer Coggin, the furniture company—that this piece came to be. Bizarre by American standards, the sofa shown on the bottom here and other pieces in Thayer Coggin's "Prisma" collection are said to be selling surprisingly well.

This Dallas living room boasts an intriguing combination of furniture, including two Memphis pieces—the sofa and the "Schwarzenberg" table by Hans Hollein. The lamps beside the sofa are the sort of cool, impersonal Italian designs Memphis has tried to get away from. Surprisingly enough, the two Italian styles blend together quite well.

While Memphis has consciously tried to rebel against Modern design, its "Lido" sofa works very well in combination with two Le Corbusier chairs that epitomize the Modern style. The two black chairs, designed by Josef Hoffmann, recall a design period with which Memphis has more sympathy—that is, the Viennese design of the early 1900s.

chapter 4

Of all the Memphis and Memphis-inspired pieces, the tables can be least faulted for impracticality. Their colors, of course, are often unusually bright. Their proportions can seem absurd (needlessly bulky legs, overly elaborate bases, and so on). Their forms are unfamiliar. Yet few fail to function as tables. Nor do they ask us to reassess our notions of what a table should be, even though their sometimes ludicrous features do encourage us to take less seriously the social rituals we perform around them.

The most fanciful are the coffee tables. Ever since the fifties, creating a coffee-table base has offered designers a chance to fling all concepts of functionality to the winds and realize their most far-out sculptural fantasies. Memphis carries on in this proud tradition, blithely ignoring the chrome-and-glass coffee table imperative that has taken part in one sleek Modern interior after another. *These* coffee tables are true "conversation pieces"— whimsical, surprising, with bases of marble or wood covered in plastic laminate that bring to mind pieces in childhood board games, cartoonish machines, or miniature cities with fantastic architecture. They can serve as effective foils for furniture that is either more seriously Modern, more seriously traditional, or more seriously rundown than the table itself.

Functional though these tables are, they make perhaps the most convincing case for regarding Memphis, together with its offshoots and parallels, as "art furniture." The coffee table, called upon to do so little, can *afford* to be art. With this in mind, you might do well to purchase a Memphis or Memphis-inspired coffee table, since it is bound to be much more interesting than anything America's big, timid furniture manufacturers are cranking out these days. What's more, these tables can bring life to the sort of comfortable but visually boring upholstered Modern pieces that are often the sole possibility for Americans wishing to furnish their living rooms in a contemporary manner.

Memphis' occasional and end tables are less fanciful than the coffee tables. Some could even pass as near-conventional Modern pieces, though Michele de Lucchi's "Kristall," looking like a too-cute-for-words extraterrestrial, is not one of them. Materials, rather than bizarre forms, often provide the visual interest— for instance, Shiro Kuramata's simple and very lovely "Kyoto" and "Nara" tables, made of a combination of white cement and bits of multicolored glass, look like a cross between terrazzo and nougat candy.

The dining tables are, for the most part, straightforward. Aside from their patterned plastic laminate tops, they do not differ radically from typical four-legged rec-

The library in Rainer Krause's home in Bad Essen, West Germany, boasts Ettore Sottsass' "Cantone" table, which the designer created for Zanotta, an Italian furniture company. (Note that, while the look of this table, as well as that of many other pieces in this book can be termed "Memphis," in fact they are produced by manufacturers other than Memphis itself, though conceived by designers associated with Memphis itself.) This room also includes Matteo Thun's "Bouquet for Six Flowers" design for the German manufacturer Anthologie Quartett, as well as Thun's "Chad" coffeepot and "Onega" cups, which are from Memphis. The silver plate was designed by Sottsass not for Memphis but for Officina Alessi, another Italian manufacturer of stylish contemporary design objects. This up-to-the-second room, incidentally, is in an old castle, Schloss Huennefeld.

TABLES

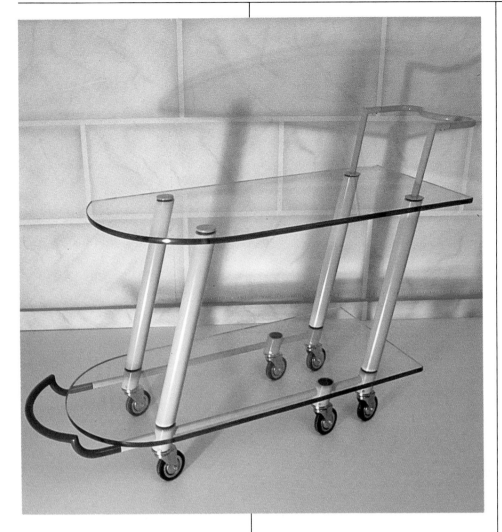

Javier Mariscal, one of the leading young designers in Barcelona, a city that rivals Milan in its experimental approach to design, created the "Hilton" trolley (left) for Memphis' 1981 collection. Its shelves are made of gray smoked glass, its structure of painted metal. Of all the Memphis pieces, this one has given rise to perhaps the largest number of knockoffs.

This California kitchen (right) boasts, aside from its sensible and functional arrangement of built-in cabinets, a contrastingly whimsical table by Los Angeles furniture artist Peter Shire. The table, very close in spirit and look to the Memphis pieces, is proof positive that such furniture need not always be relegated to artwork status and never used in daily life.

tangular dining tables. There are, however, exceptions: tables with cumbersome bases, or bases that leave no room for people's legs or feet, or ones structured so that fewer people can sit around them than their sizable tops might lead you to believe. With these, we enter the realm pinpointed by English design historian Penny Sparke, in which semiuseless furniture meets the needs of no one but "rich pop stars and fashion designers who can afford to indulge in their fantasies." Why *not* buy a table at which hardly anyone can sit when you can afford to buy a hundred more tables that can seat a dozen each? These pieces, more than any others, appear to be what many accuse *all* of Memphis and its ilk of being: rebellion against functionality for rebellion's sake.

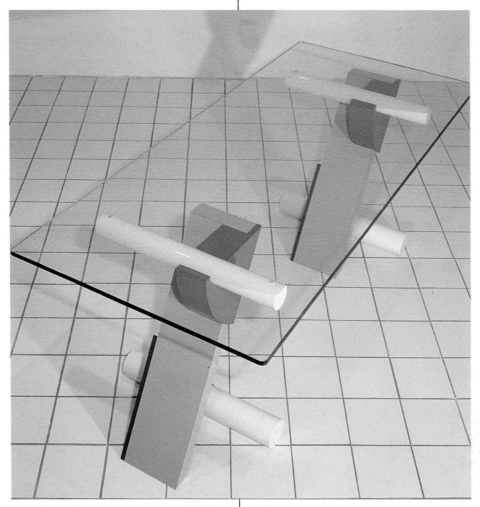

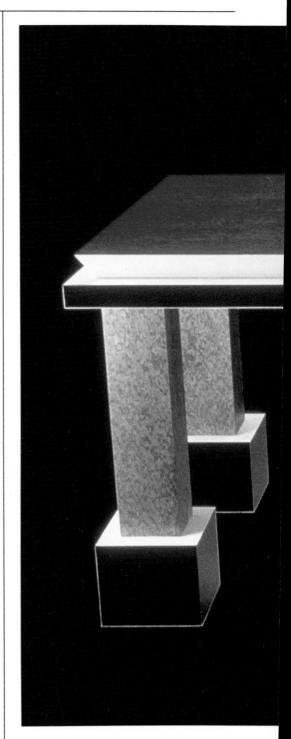

While Michele de Lucchi seems to have a predilection for cartoonlike forms, the two doodads that form the base of his "Fortune" table do not take away from this piece's ability to blend in with various types of decor. With its glass top, the table does not call that much attention to itself. Indeed, one could easily imagine its weird legs getting lost (or almost lost) in a room full of Victorian or Mission pieces, a far cry from its origins in the Memphis 1982 collection.

Memphis' 1984 collection includes the "Palm Springs" table, designed by Ettore Sottsass. In keeping with his interest in the ritualistic function of certain pieces of furniture in Western society today, Sottsass has given this table a monumental quality. The connotation of quality comes, perhaps, from its thick top and blocky, overscaled legs, each of which rests on an absurdly outsized base. Sturdiness and strength are embodied in the design.

Ettore Sottsass' "Metro" sideboard (left), from Memphis' 1983 collection, is made of typically contradictory materials: metal, plastic laminate, marble, and aluminum. Its clear-cut diagonals go off in all directions, and the whole thing looks as if it could collapse in a second—which of course it won't, Sottsass being the seasoned industrial designer that he is.

"Madonna," (above) from Memphis' 1984 collection, was designed by the architects of Arquitectonica, one of America's most inventive and successful young architectural firms. Like Memphis, Arquitectonica likes to parody the forms and colors of Pop architecture. This particular table takes off on the idea of the kidney-shaped swimming pool, that staple of Miami hotel architecture of the fifties (not so coincidentally, Arquitectonica itself is based in the Miami area).

David Zelman's spindly buffet table, designed in 1983, is ideal for somewhat cramped spaces. Airy, open-framed furniture that lets the space flow is preferable to larger, more visually cumbersome pieces.

"Belvedere," a handsome, small table made of black-and-white granite, black-veined and black marble, and serena stone, was designed by Aldo Cibic for Memphis' 1982 collection. The table's bright red drawer is made of lacquered wood.

chapter 5

Memphis storage pieces can be grouped into two categories: those whose function and appearance, despite their unusual colors, patterns, and materials, bear a distinct resemblance to more conventional furniture; and those which, quite apart from their unusual colors, patterns, and materials, look like no furniture anyone has ever seen. There are cupboards and sideboards in or on which tableware can be stored or displayed, bookshelves and bookcases in which books can be arranged in the usual manner, chests of drawers in which clothing can be neatly tucked away, and a massive dressing table, designed by American architect Michael Graves, that would satisfy the storage needs of the most vain, most cosmetics-addicted fashion plate (see Chapter Six).

But then there are the most characteristic Memphis pieces—especially such *tours de force* as Ettore Sottsass' "Casablanca," "Carlton," "Suvretta," and "Beverly;" Masanori Umeda's robotoid "Ginza;" Shiro Kuramata's "Zambia;" Arata Isozaki's "Fuji;" and Gerard Taylor's "Le Palme"—which defy all expectations of what storage pieces should be. Some of these pieces have too few drawers placed too high up. On others, the shelves curve or slant at crazy, inconvenient angles. In some cases, such eccentricities seem justified. The "Suvretta" bookcase, for example, has cockeyed dividers, which seem plausible and are a witty answer to the problem of books which, when ranged along a shelf, always seem to end up tilting in one direction or another rather than standing up straight. Others, however, are more intractable, like the "Carlton" room divider—a weird hybrid of stylized person and stylized tree, most of whose surface space is unusable.

In fact, many of the more outlandish pieces *are* more or less unusable, at least in any conventional manner. To begin with, they are large-scaled and would make sense only in the most spacious interiors. Indeed, those interiors would *have* to be spacious to accommodate a Memphis sideboard that could hold next to nothing and another manufacturer's sideboard that could hold everything else. Given the obvious impracticality of these pieces, it seems unlikely that anyone would want to spend a huge amount of money on one; though, in fact, several happen to be among the pricier items in the Memphis catalog. Possibly, these limited production pieces of extreme design are to be regarded more as art objects and are meant to appeal solely to wealthy collectors rather than to people seeking to furnish their homes.

STORAGE PIECES

Ettore Sottsass' imposing "Carlton" is the centerpiece of Memphis' premiere collection. The colorful structure is billed as a room divider with bookshelves and two drawers. Made of wood covered with various, brightly-hued plastic laminates, it can be completely disassembled—a definite plus, if you bear in mind its considerable size. A weird hybrid of stylized person and tree, it has gained much popularity.

But consider Ettore Sottsass' outrageous "Carlton" more closely. Sottsass has said, "You have to live with furniture. It should not only surround you." Is he suggesting that if we choose to live with "Carlton," we should somehow let it shape our lives? Although this notion may seem irritating and dictatorial, it might be refreshing to own a

bookcase capable of holding just so much. A bookcase like that would force any bibliophile to simplify his or her library, to pare it down to its essentials. These carefully selected books would then fill up the shelves of "Carlton," that magical, totemlike object, which would perhaps endow them with all the unity, radiance, and magic they have in the reader's mind.

Everyone could select an ideal library—and the ideal life to go with it. The making of such an ideal library—a project inspired by the idiosyncratic, impractical, and supposedly useless "Carlton" room divider—might prove to be more fruitful an undertaking than anyone would surmise.

This response, however, springs from the more hermetic side of Memphis' storage pieces. The pieces also have a more public, more straightforwardly communicative aspect. For if Memphis storage pieces vary in their

This futuristic setting shows off to their best advantage two pieces in American designer Milo Baughman's "Prisma" collection: an étagère and a sofa. Thayer Coggin, the collection's manufacturer, took a risk with this adventurous collection. In fact, it turns out to be capturing consumers' imaginations. These colorful pieces of furniture could easily be found in an up-to-date home. The flat-textured carpet and bare walls shown here make an ideal backdrop for furniture with such presence.

degree of practicality, all exhibit the same revolutionary and highly communicative use of materials and color. In these pieces, materials and colors do not simply exist, they also serve as signs that convey meaning and a particular attitude about living in the world as it is today.

The most important of these materials is undoubtedly the boldly patterned plastic laminates that have come to be so closely identified with the Memphis state of mind. As Italian journalist Barbara Radice notes, prior to Memphis, plastic laminate—"the symbol of suburbia"—had been relegated to kitchens, bathrooms, and children's rooms, as well as the interiors of such inelegant public places as roadside fast-food chains. The material suggested not wealth or social status but "vulgarity, poverty, and bad taste." In their desire to wreck hierarchies in design (and, implicitly, in society), Memphis chose to bring "bad taste," in the guise of garish plastic laminates, into the living room and dining room—interiors often given over to ostentation and opulence. Many Memphis storage pieces are intended for those very interiors. Gaudy and hard to ignore, they get the point across quite clearly—a point only strengthened when Sottsass, in his "Metro" sideboard, combines plastic laminate with that epitome of opulence, marble. Paradoxically, although their plastic laminate finishes evoke mass taste, the presence of these storage pieces in a living room or dining room may not shatter the hierarchies Sottsass and his followers would like to abolish, since Memphis is invariably coming to be accepted as "good taste" in its own right.

The colors of these storage pieces, like those that grace so much of Memphis' output, also links them to Pop design. They smack—deliciously—of the cheap, the artificial, the saccharine and of the rickety Modernism of the Third World. In this way, they thumb their noses at the austere, muted tones of "Good Design" and at almost all European furniture ever designed, most of which lacked such high color. With their vast range and improbable combinations of colors, patterns, and shapes, they draw many co-

The "Casablanca" sideboard, designed by Ettore Sottsass, is made of wood covered with the sort of loud, weirdly patterned plastic laminates that first put Memphis on the map. Its central portion contains shelves for storage, as well as three drawers and a tilting door. Its resemblance to a totem figure is not accidental.

existing cultures together into individual pieces: here a red right out of Burger King, there a gelatolike peachy cream, with some violent violet from a West African textile, and a hot yellow straight out of a graffiti artist's spray can. So much for hierarchies! Instead, we have a sense of joyful plurality, all the television channels in the world playing at once.

Many American "art furniture" storage pieces display a similarly adventurous use of materials and colors. Some even compare in terms of impracticality. But larger furniture manufacturers are now trying their hands at Memphis-like storage pieces, with somewhat less dazzling results. It seems that, once the possibility of reaching a mass market arises, American designers are wary of

"Fuji," a pair of small dressing units designed by leading Japanese architect Arata Isozaki, boasts open, oddly shaped shelves, two doors with internal drawer units, and mirrors. The finish is reminiscent of the sort of spray-painted graffiti that decorates subway trains in New York City. These pieces were included in Memphis' 1981 collection.

taking the sort of big risks Memphis has taken. The forms they come up with are not quite eccentric enough, the colors more heavy-handed, and the combinations predictable. Of course, these pieces are more reasonably priced than the Italian ones and, if you happen to live in the United States, can be obtained more easily. In eschewing the most extreme of Memphis' mannerisms, they also turn out to be

more usable—a factor very much in their favor.

But while the appearance of such adventurous furniture bodes well for the terminally sluggish, conservative American furniture industry, the pieces themselves are, to be blunt, watered-down versions of brilliant originals—an ironic outcome, given that the originals play off a style meant to *please* the masses.

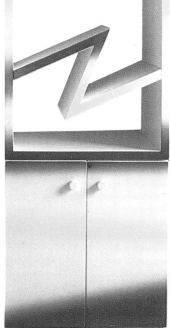

"Ginza" (left),which Japanese designer Masanori Umeda created for the Memphis 1982 collection, is more playful than functional with its robotoid shape complete with a "chest" of drawers. A piece like this would be most appropriate in a home with at least a few extra square feet, where it can take up floor space without cutting into necessary— and functional —storage space.

George J. Sowden's "D'Antibes" (below left), a small cabinet with two doors and two shelves, boasts bright primary colors. Its long, slim legs and high body make it ideal for rooms where, to keep space flowing, furniture should be raised well above the floor.

Painted basswood and erector set parts were combined by American designer Edward Zucca in his 1981, punningly titled, "Middleboy" (below). Like the Memphis " robot," Zucca's storage piece brings new interest to a category of furniture that, thanks to the Modernist penchant for built-ins, seemed due for extinction. Modern design favors solutions, like built-ins, that are applicable to both large and small spaces. Memphis, in its defiance of standardization, prefers designs that cannot be used just anywhere. Accordingly, Zucca's "Middleboy" is most appropriate for larger rooms, and it is too space-consuming for smaller ones.

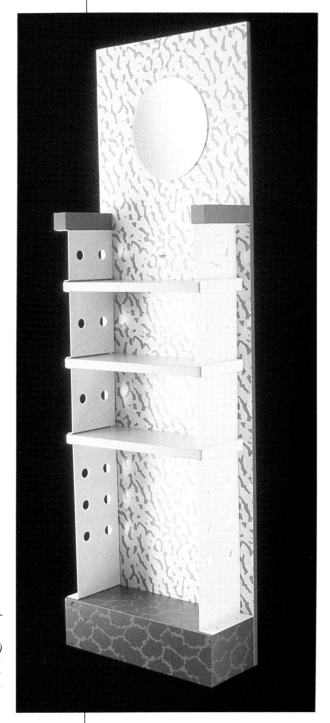

Ettore Sottsass' "Beverly" sideboard (above) from Memphis' 1981 collection—one of his most radical and interesting pieces—is made of plastic laminate and natural briar. The useless little bulb— a motif that figures in several of Sottsass' designs from this period— adds to the carnival air that surrounds this weird piece.

Shelves of metal and boldly patterned plastic laminate (right) distinguish "Coral," one of designer Nathalie du Pasquier's contributions to Memphis' 1984 collection. The contrast of materials marks a more refined statement within a single piece of furniture than has been seen in many of its predecessors.

chapter 6

Many people dismiss all of Memphis as extravagant and impractical. This is, of course, a generalization. Also, given Memphis' aims, questions of practicality may be beside the point. However, Memphis—and here we come to an area virtually no Memphis-imitators have entered —does offer three spectacular (and spectacularly expensive) pieces that are more *folies des grandeurs* than furniture. As such, they deserve a category of their own.

Two of these ultraluxurious showpieces of craftspersons' art constitute American architect Michael Graves' contribution to the project. One is the weighty "Plaza," an Art Deco-ish dressing table which, with its base, body, and head, Graves writes, "aspires to resee the artifact as replica both of building and of man." The other is the even more opulent "Stanhope" single bed, in bird's-eye maple veneer with decorations in lacquered wood, mirror, and miniature lamps in brass and glass.

It is interesting to note that the Memphis "look" can include these pieces, although they relate more to Graves' recent architecture than to anything Sottsass and his associates have created. Graves may well have been invited to participate in Memphis not only because of his originality as a designer but also to provide the fledgling company's roster with a prestigious, internationally known, and much-hyped "big name." Yet this American architect's concern with the relationship between people and the objects with which they surround themselves certainly links up with similar concerns of the Italian designers who form Memphis' core.

The third piece, Japanese designer Masanori Umeda's "Tawaraya," is even more unlikely: a wooden boxing ring, its floor covered with a tatami mat, the ring furnished with silk cushions and a wooden tray. "Tawaraya" is meant not to show off Rocky's latest antics but to serve as a conversation "pit." Indeed, the design wittily points up several contradictory aspects of conversation: its rational, polite, civilized quality (as evoked by the delicately colored pillows, and a tatami that recalls the tranquillity of Japan's traditional domestic interiors); its undercurrents of competitiveness and irrational hostility; and its inevitable, overt clashes of will against will (as evoked by the boxing ring itself). This piece of conceptual furniture is, obviously, not for everyone. Still, like so much of Memphis' furniture, its mere existence is challenging and thought-provoking. It does what Memphis at its best intends to do: to be beautiful and, at the same time, clear the haze of received notions through which we view our society.

For Memphis' premiere collection, Japanese designer Masanori Umeda created "Tawaraya," a wooden boxing ring with a black-and-white striped border. The floor is a tatami mat. The cushions are of delicately colored silk. The piece can be used in large, open interiors; it is especially good for people given to internecine feuding but who have not lost their sense of humor about it.

PIECES
DE RÉSISTANCE

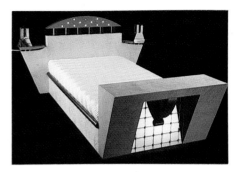

While American architect Michael Graves' furniture is rather more sedate than many other Memphis pieces, his "Stanhope" bed, from the 1982 collection, provides a handsome foil for the collection's zanier designs. The bed is made of extremely luxurious materials and sports an astronomical price tag.

Though not as opulent as the Michael Graves designs for Memphis, this plastic-laminate-covered bed (below) carries certain Memphis propensities: odd, cheap-looking colors and intentionally klutzy-looking forms. Such a one-of-a-kind bed requires a good deal of space around it, so its full effect can be appreciated. Architect Vincas Meilus is this piece's creator.

The pièce de résistance at left is really the interior architecture of the space. Its design—the work of Jean-Pierre Fenez and Jean-Michel Venay of the French firm cabinet Laur—proves how a Memphis design (the Nathalie du Pasquier fabric on the seating units) can work in a rich or spare room.

American architect Michael Graves' "Plaza" dressing table with stool, (above), from Memphis' 1981 collection, includes a stool, a tilting mirror, six drawers in painted wood and natural briar, and decorative small mirrors and low-voltage light bulbs. The Art Deco overtones of this piece are more characteristic of Graves' work than they are of most Memphis designs.

Memphis' parallels to the decorative design movements of the early twentieth century are most evident in its own line of decorative objects—some functional, others purely ornamental—in ceramic, porcelain, wood, silver, and blown glass. These embody what designer Andrea Branzi terms "the new craftsmanship," one that opposes the repetitiveness of mass production with handmade (and therefore expensive), one-of-a-kind pieces, most of which rely on traditional craft methods. Curiously, Branzi insists that handcrafting is *not* an alternative to industrial production. Rather, he sees it as a kind of research, as "industry's 'specialized laboratory.'" Some American manufacturers may agree, for if Memphis has only begun to have an impact on this country's mass-produced furniture, there are already countless decorative objects—especially vases, tableware, and glassware, all produced in fairly large quantities—that show a clear Memphis influence (and which, incidentally, are much more affordable than the originals, though somewhat less beautifully crafted).

The sheer range of Memphis' own decorative objects is impressive. It includes ashtrays, teapots, cups, bowls, goblets, vases, and miscellaneous table accessories. The diversity of shapes and colors is overwhelming. Even the more functional items—the tea-half-animal, that zoologists have yet to classify.

With these objects, a designer's imagination enjoys free rein, since they are small and need not adhere to ergonomic guidelines. Unlike a chair which, to be saleable, really must have a back and a seat and be able to accommodate a person, with these decorative objects, there is rarely any need to choose one shape over another. Indeed, a particular shape is often chosen for no reason at all but that it may have seemed fun at the time or struck the designer's fancy. This rationale may sound self-indulgent. In fact, it is responsible for the endlessly pleasing freshness, humor, and unpretentiousness of these decorative pieces.

CERAMICS, GLASS, SILVER

Ettore Sottsass' stunning silver fruit bowl, "Murmansk," costs thousands of dollars. Even though Sottsass argues against hierarchies, he and the other Memphis designers are obviously seduced by the possibility of creating visually beautiful objects that go beyond the most extravagant dreams of luxury— and are strictly for the very *rich.*

pots, for example—boast fantastic forms that, without impeding their usefulness, lend them a fantastic air: of vessels from other worlds, of wondrous tools made by a vanished civilization that left no clue as to their use, or of small creatures, half-building

And so, with these extremely appealing objects—some perfect for teatime, others ideal for more or less formal dinner parties, and still others purely ornamental— we leave the adult world behind and enter one of purest nonsense. Like Memphis lamps,

Unidentifiable as it may at first appear, Marco Zanini's "Rigel," from the 1982 Memphis collection, is in fact a bowl made of blue, black, red, and clear glass. Its lid and stem, also of glass, are obviously functional. The little conical appendage sticking out from its left side is just for fun.

these objects encourage us to daydream. And even more purposefully than those lamps, these objects take us further into that reverie. The sole purpose of, say, Sottsass' "Euphrates" may be to dream: The dishes are coming! They are alive and friendly. They stand on each other's shoulders like gymnasts, topple over, rise up again, say "OK, let's see if we really can break this time." Now they are descending on the refrigerator to liberate the food—Indian pastries in pastel colors, leftover lasagna, and grapes. "Alcor" may help invent another unreal landscape: A green powder is used for this particular ritual; bald priests got up in ancient Egyptian garb sidle down corridors inside the pyramid, all in a flurry over the ritual, yet trying to appear calm and dignified. Everyone believes in the green powder. The walls are decorated with murals featuring people using it in a variety of ways, some funny, others frightening or incomprehensible. The air smells; from an inner sanctum, puffs of pinkish-orange smoke emerge. Thun's "Great Lakes" series, useful as tableware, is reverie-inducing, too: Strange day at our farm. The hens are laying eggs, but the eggs come out with roosters' combs on them. Brother goes out in the year of the "little farm," the one that's like our farm used to be before agribusiness took over. He starts juggling a few of these mutant eggs, but they never come back down; they just

This medley of American manufactured and designed tableware and bar accessories suggests just how widespread Memphis' influence has become outside of Europe. The pieces are: (clockwise) architect Laurinda Spear's buffet plate for Swid Powell; Sasaki's ice bucket for the "Prisma" collection; a glass from Toscany by Claudia Schwide; a cup and plate from Mary-James Inc.'s "Alpha 3 Dinnerware"; a wine glass and a bar glass, both from Sasaki's "Prisma" collection; and a tabletop gift from Hutschenreuther.

Sigma was one of the first American manufacturers to pick up on what Memphis was doing. Their Memphis-like patterns and shapes are made in much larger quantities than the Memphis originals; these plates and mugs are more reasonably priced as well.

fly straight up into the air. Someone hiding behind a haystack urges low, burping sounds out of an amplified contrabassoon. "No omelettes today, I guess," though there are always powdered eggs...

To return to reality the American offshoots of these marvelous pieces are somewhat less subtle than the Memphis originals, and less rich in associations. Yet they too offer a welcome alternative to the plainer, more severe Modern pieces we have become accustomed to; and they avoid both mindless retromania and forced obscure references to past architectural styles. As such, they will not fail to impart a certain freshness and vitality to any room of your home—and give you something to wonder at, some late afternoon in August, on a day that already reminds you of what Septembers are like, with the sky cloudless and blue, and outside the window the river's reflection shimmering gold upon the glass facade of a building whose purpose is as yet obscure to you, as obscure as "Alioth" or "Rigel" or "Cassiopeia"... an obscurity that makes it beautiful, even if you never do find out its "true" meaning.

Marco Zanini's "Cassiopeia" glass (above), in clear, blue, and aquamarine hues is almost too beautiful to actually drink from; it has a more ceremonial than functional air to it. The whole idea that Memphis' objects can be used in a ritualistic way—even in made-up rituals that have nothing to do with organized religion—may strike people as pretentious. In fact, it is not so much real rituals as the possibility of—and impossibility of— ritual that the designer wishes to suggest.

Memphis' 1982 collection included Marco Zanini's "Baykal" (left), a flower vase in turned ceramic with a stylized ceramic "flower." Like many of the Memphis pieces, this one reinstates the notion of the decorative object, which Modern design, with its emphasis on the purely functional, rejected.

Peter Shire's ceramic teapot stems from a similarly freewheeling way of thinking. When asked about what he thought economic activity would be like in a present-day Eden, Shire replied that it would consist primarily of "... pottery exchange. The pots would be made in pottery towns. The pots themselves would be of a very high level, very refined, no crocks. Pottery would be both product and activity."

Marek Cecula, a ceramicist living in the United States, made his "Reconstruction of Paradise" of vitrified china. This strange minimonument (it is only 33 inches high at its pinnacle) needs a large room to exude its magnetic pull. The piece has a templelike quality. The only problem: nobody knows what religion the "temple" was built for. According to Memphis, this not-knowing is not a problem.

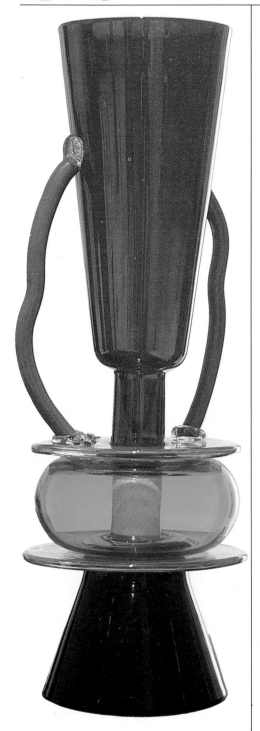

Variously colored blown glass distinguishes Ettore Sottsass' "Sirio" (far left), from Memphis' 1982 collection. The photograph does not give a sense of how delicately scaled the piece is—so delicately scaled that the squiggly handles of this vase take on a vulnerable quality, which makes one want to touch the piece as gently as one would a small, exotic bird. Bruce Lenore's "Gray Jar," (left) executed in raku, has a rather more robust appearance. Indeed, one can often tell American pieces apart from the Memphis objects that inspired them by their scale, which tends to be chunkier.

Bruce Lenore's "Magic" (above), a raku piece that measures 26 inches by 14 inches by 5 inches, has loud colors reminiscent of some of the Memphis designs. Its zigzagging forms lend it an air of science fantasy. Or you might imagine its mirroring shapes are two ancient Egyptian pharoahs conversing about arcane matters that we of the 1980s will never understand. (The parameters of Memphis-style logic could easily include a conversation between, say, Akhnaten and his son King Tut, who could actually never have had an adult conversation together.)

Andrea Branzi's "Labrador" sauceboat is made of silver and glass, and was included in Memphis' 1982 collection. Branzi, one of the guiding lights behind Studio Alchymia as well as Memphis, creates highly idiosyncratic pieces that belie the misconception that Memphis designers must follow a particular party line.

Everything we do," says Ettore Sottsass, "is dedicated to life and not to eternity"—a statement that can be taken as the Memphis *cri de coeur*. In light of this, Memphis' electronic objects—its televisions, clocks, and several still-unrealized projects, all of them objects that shape our notion of the movement of life in our fast-paced contemporary world—can be seen as the purest metaphors for what this design movement is all about. For Memphis seeks to be thoroughly of that fast-paced world. Its forms, colors, and patterns are not meant to be valid forever—only as valid as today's news is valid for today. Indeed, that its electronic objects (as well as many of its other designs) will surely assume a "dated" look in ten years' time does not (at least to my thinking) diminish their value but adds to their appeal. It gives them the air of snapshots, perhaps a bit clunky or inartistic; clumsy as our own attempts to capture photographically or otherwise, something fleeting. Or else these objects (especially the clocks) can be seen as memorials to what cannot be memorialized—that is, time in its endless passage.

On a lighter note, the Memphis designers take a far more irreverent approach to electronics than did earlier designers. After World War II, when electronic equipment for the home first became widely available, industrial designers presented these consumables in one of two guises. They either endowed them with a heavily technological look that featured drab, "serious" colors and visible functioning parts, or they tried to make the equipment blend in with the home environment by giving it the look of furniture, as was the case with the massive television consoles of the mid-1950s; these camouflaged television's technological innards with period frou-frou.

Memphis, however, takes a third route, more akin to that explored by such American designers of the thirties as Raymond Loewy, Russel Wright, and Walter Dorwin Teague, who created what at the time was labeled "packaging" for electronic equipment; for example, a streamlined shell which hid a radio's working parts also glamorized its function, so that the radio was transformed into a prop for the futuristic romance that was supposed to be daily life.

Half a century later, Memphis' version of the future is quite different from that advanced by the creators of this streamlined style, for whom the future was cause for unadulterated optimism. Memphis opts for today's bright, synthetic, perishable colors and hyperkinetic on-the-edge patterns rather than thirties' muted hues and rounded contours. If it refers to any past style, it is a style *way* in the past—as in some of George J. Sowden's table clocks that recall ancient Egyptian monuments with their truncated pyramidal forms. Streamlined styling gave objects a sculptural quality that

Memphis designer Nathalie du Pasquier created this clock in 1983 for a collection called "Objects for the Electronic Age." As shown throughout this book, many of du Pasquier's objects have the look of toy buildings—a conceit that works very well, given this designer's love of high-powered, dazzling, childlike bright patterns.

ELECTRONICS

chapter 8

sought to convey the essence of speed, hailed in the 1930s as *the* twentieth-century goddess. Memphis' electronic objects are much less sculptural looking. In fact, their flat surfaces, covered with colorful patterns, become decidedly decorative.

The results of this approach are both amusing and beautiful. Some manufacturers evidently think so, too, to judge by the recent appearance of equipment sheathed in colorful metals rather than the usual black, gray, or fake woodgrain.

While nowhere near as outlandish as Memphis' electronic pieces, this bright red Sony cassette unit suggests that the Italian design movement is having a noticeable effect on mass-marketed items. The emphasis on loud colors and the downplay of the technology of the furniture is typical of modern Italian design. Other, even wilder hues, have shown up on Sony items recently.

Memphis' wild patterns seem worlds apart from trimline phones with their look of sleek functionality. But in this home office, French decorators Jean-Pierre Fenez and Jean-Michel Venay of cabinet Laur included a desk enlivened by one of those patterns and a telephone for the busy businessperson who works at it. Now we have only to wait for phones that are as extreme as the rest of this room—a room that, in keeping with Memphis' anti-hierarchical stance, tries to do away with distinctions of work and play with a work environment that doesn't look serious.

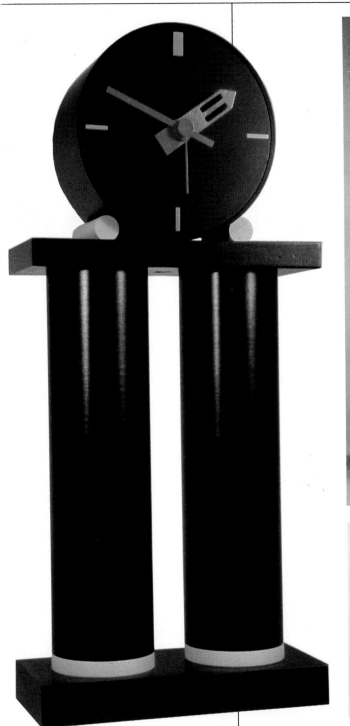

The "Eleganza" clock (far left), made of aluminum and created by English designer Keith Gibbons, measures 12½ inches high and has quartz works.

Gibbons' "Wooden Block" (above left) clock, of painted wood, has quartz works as well and stands 10 inches high. Unlike Memphis' clocks, these were designed for mass-production and are priced well within the range of many consumers—as opposed to the Memphis clocks, which are quite expensive. Both clocks are available at Hot House. With their simplified classical forms, both clocks recall pieces done in the mid-18th century in the Biedermeier style—that is, the childlike neoclassical style that developed in Germany and was named after a popular cartoon character of that period. Gibbons' designs, however, are even more simplified than the Beidermeier pieces, to the point where they seem as toylike as—though less intense than—the Memphis pieces.

Gibbons also designed the checkered ceramic "Blitz" clock (below left). The clock is made by a process known as slip molding, which calls for a plaster mold into which liquid clay is poured and then left to harden. It measures 12½ inches high by 5½ inches wide and is priced to be available to a wide public.

Memphis' 1982 collection included George J. Sowden's "Metropole" clock (right), which is made of wood finished in patterned plastic laminates. A large-scaled piece such as this one would work best in a generously proportioned interior. Indeed, its scale gives the table clock's cartoon patterns a certain seriousness not always found in Memphis' lighthearted furniture.

chapter 9

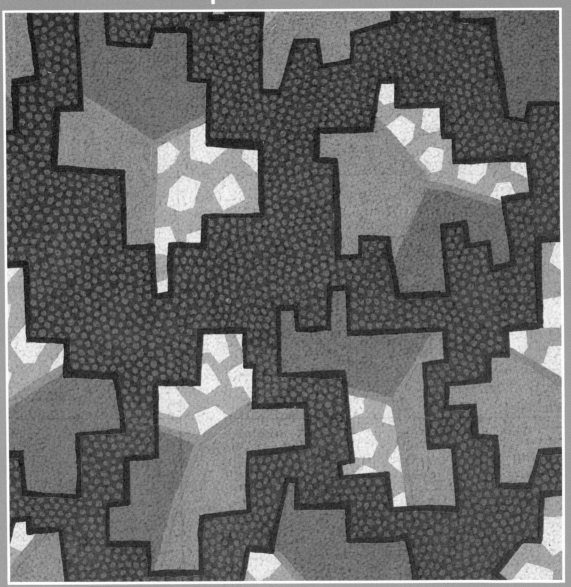

emphis patterns wiggle. Buzz. Pulse. Swarm. Whether they enliven rugs, cotton chintzes, or the plastic laminates covering individual objects or interior surfaces, these patterns never play second fiddle to form or function, and they don't blend politely into the background. Rather, they leap out at us, freak us out, keep us on our toes. And, as elements in a room's or object's design, they swallow structure in an incessant flash or undulation, or else break it up into discontinuous parts. And, unlike the blank surfaces of Modern interiors that let you focus on spatial dimensions, surfaces covered with Memphis' dense patterns vibrate to the point where the space's contours begin to blur.

The colors of these patterns vary. Some are drab—intriguingly so—with an electronic tang to them, like the spectrum of grays in a black-and-white television's static pattern. Others are shockingly bright; in their intensity they recall both the colors seen in video games and those found in traditional African, Mexican, and Indian fabrics—this, an instance of Memphis' emphasis on convergences between present and past (evident in the name "Memphis" itself). Still other patterns, in black and white, recall Op Art or the covers of some graphics that advertise supermarket sales. There are Memphis patterns that look like half-baked imitations of flagstone or terrazzo, that evoke television sets on the blink, their picture tubes blizzards of zigzags and ripples; that mimic the blunt, bold supergraphics of road signs on superhighways or designs never meant to be visually pleasing in the first place, on manhole covers, metal cellar doors, wire garbage baskets, or inside "protective" envelopes. Other patterns have a more exotic air, offering a mix of jagged comic strip *Zaps* and *Pows* and asymmetrical polygons reminiscent of traditional African textiles.

By bringing this barrage of associations into the home—a barrage not unlike what hits you each time you turn on the television or open a newspaper—Memphis designers tame our world, joke about it, and so make it seem ridiculous, something not to get all *that* upset about. For instance, Ettore Sottsass' pre-Memphis "Bacterio" plastic laminate brings to mind some hard-to-decipher newspaper photo, the kind that accompanies an article about the latest incurable disease menacing mankind.

That article, written in bland, seamless "newspaperese," seems to make a lot of sense. But then, reading it more closely reveals how much has been left out, how much there is between the lines.

PATTERNS

Memphis designers George J. Sowden and Nathalie du Pasquier collaborated on two extraordinary carpets—"Floating" and "Calculus"—for Steeles Carpets, an English manufacturer. Shown here is "Floating." While a whole room carpeted in a hyperactive Memphis pattern could be a little hard on the eyes, carpets like this one could work very effectively when used as area rugs. Rooms most suitable for patterns like this are ones where the background carpeting is flat, commercial, and in a darker color, against which vibrant hues could glisten.

grade school notebooks. Earth tones and neutrals are rare. Indeed, there is nothing natural about these hues: like so much of Memphis, they allude to the "ugly," more synthetic aspects of contemporary civilization.

The sources for Memphis' animated patterns come from all over. Microbes seen wriggling and multiplying through a microscope's lens could be a metaphor for one pattern, while others bring to mind the frankly attention-grabbing, inartistic

Look twice at that picture and you realize that you have no real idea what these squiggly lines have to do with your life. Suddenly the whole newspaper becomes a thin disguise for chaos and complexity. The photo of soldiers on a bridge in El Salvador, the photo of a bullet-riddled McDonald's; even the more innocuous photo of two people holding hands and sitting on a park bench—all are presented as examples of "typical vignettes" that sum up this or that facet of reality. But if you ask yourself whether they add up to a meaningful picture of today's world, the answer, of course, is No. No matter how many newspaper photos are jammed onto a page, they never add up to a totality.

Cannon's Sterling Choice line, created by Richard Kitchen, offers these Memphis-like sheets. In fact, the pattern is more reminiscent of New Wave graphics, which in turn recalls the graphics of the Russian constructivists. But no one cares about who has got what avant-garde credentials when it comes to sleep. Whatever the inspiration, these colorful sheets can add plenty of zip to a bedroom—especially a child's room.

The English company Steeles Carpets Ltd. offers "Calculus," an 80 percent wool, 20 percent nylon contract-grade carpeting designed by George J. Sowden and Nathalie du Pasquier. This durable carpeting suggests that functionality need not be forgotten even if the designers are intent on including vivid pattern in a textile.

We cannot *know* the totality. With that as a given—and it is, I think, a given Memphis takes very much for granted—the world comes to seem overwhelmingly and terrifyingly incomprehensible. There is a great deal that you do not *and cannot* know about the conditions that determine your life. There is a great deal about microbes, soldiers, and lovers that you will never know. But turn that photograph of those deadly microbes into a plastic laminate pattern, use it to cover a shelf in your house, and somehow you have become light-hearted about all this craziness, have accepted what novelist Mi-

lan Kundera calls "the unbearable lightness of being." Indeed, colored with some particularly silly hue, microbes become positively laughable (though we never forget their ability to kill us).

Similar thinking seems to underlie Memphis' African-inspired textile patterns. Westerners may occasionally wax romantic about Africa, but in many ways that continent still represents the Unknown. Memphis' African-inspired patterns do not so much make light of the Third World as they welcome it inside, refuse to shut it out, want us to acknowledge that we who buy Memphis and put it in our Western homes

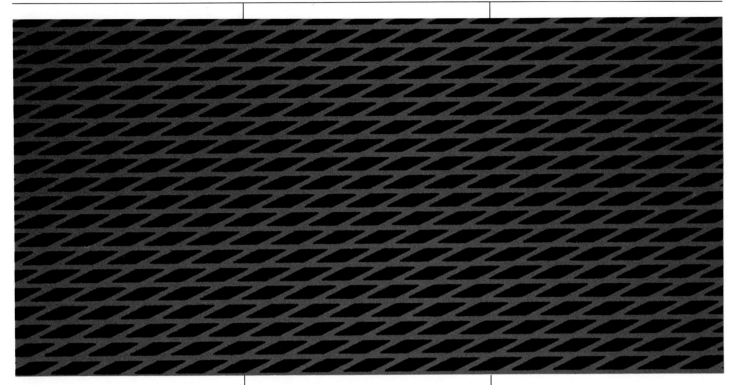

are living in the same world as the people of Chad, Nigeria, and Zaire.

There is also the purely visual side of Memphis, as opposed to this more theoretical (though essential) one. In a spirit of literal-mindedness, we can say that Memphis and Memphis-inspired plastic laminates will add zip to any room and, of course, are as washable as any plastic laminate. Given that Memphis' laminates can be purchased in sheets, and used on furniture or built-ins you either make yourself or have made for you, they can be used effectively to cover, say, a kitchen or bathroom counter, or—if you want to be truer to the Memphis spirit—a simple, custom-made

bookcase or the exterior of a chest of drawers. Like Memphis' furniture and objects, its patterned plastic laminates need not play a central role in an interior. Employed judiciously, they can make their point and add bounce to a room as well.

The fabrics and carpets are more flamboyant, both in their colors and patterns. Nathalie du Pasquier's rugs in particular are quite overpowering—over-poweringly beautiful, too—and would probably have to be handled with care and combined with other elements only after careful consideration. With these, simple, solid-toned pieces of furniture might work best, so that the exuberant pattern on the

"Rete 2" (above), a plastic laminate pattern designed by Ettore Sottsass, recalls, in its weavelike motif, the wire garbage baskets one sees on city streetcorners—a typical reference to the nondesign of today's urban environments. The kitchen (right) in Rainer Krause's home in West Germany, features a built-in refrigerator whose door is covered with a plastic laminate designed by Paola Navone for Abet Laminati/ Driade. Navone was a member of Memphis' Studio Alchymia.

floor can show to best advantage. Fabrics can be used sparingly, to cover accent pillows, say—a concept that many people like. And since Memphis aims to do away with the tacky/tasteful distinction along with all others, why not?

Created for Memphis 1983 collection, Nathalie du Pasquier designed this "California" rug (far left), made of handwoven wool. It is characteristic of this designer's highly original use of pattern and color. A piece like this could define a seating area, but it could also serve as a piece of artwork, and look stunning just hanging on a wall with lots of empty space around it. "California," along with Memphis' other rugs, is among that company's most successful creations.

American artist Keith Haring's pictographic patterns (left) seem to have inspired a number of Memphis designers. The 1983 "Untitled," like most of Haring's output, has a swarming, hopped-up energy that comes out of New York's own hyperactivity. Memphis' designs are not cheap, but they are less expensive than a Haring these days.

Considering the wide array of Memphis' patterns, you might find this Sottsass carpet design (following page) one of the more extreme motifs of the style. It brings to mind the "theme" carpets one sees in Middle America's cocktail lounges and bowling alley restaurants—interiors where the floor coverings are usually half-hidden thanks to dim lighting and where they are used as much to hide dirt as to provide a decorative motif. Sottsass' carpet might be fun in a home media center.

Gerard Taylor's "Oregon" rug (left inset), of handwoven wool, bears a certain affinity to the austere paintings of Joseph Albers. The slightly "off" colors, however, are pure Memphis. Less wild than some other Memphis designs, "Oregon" could work well in a living room with mainly Modern furnishings. It would, however, need touches of color that Modern design often lacks.

"Tortue" (background), a 100 percent polyester fabric from the French company Yves Gonnet, features a pattern of what look like inkspots on a deep red background. In the Memphis spirit, it turns a mishap— spilled ink—into a pattern, one way of taming the disorderly world while still admitting that it can't be tamed.

Right inset, top to bottom Nathalie du Pasquier's "Craquele" plastic laminate pattern, from the 1983 Memphis collection, looks like an image of cells seen under a microscope. Associations like this can enliven the kinetic design. "Marmo," a plastic laminate designed by George J. Sowden for Memphis' 1983 collection, boasts a marblelike pattern so exaggerated that it could never pass for the real thing. Memphis' plastic laminates can be bought by the yard; they are just as functional (if somewhat more pricey) as other similar products. "Lamiera," a plastic laminate Ettore Sottsass designed for the 1983 Memphis collection, has the sort of bland yet buzzy quality that, for many Memphis designers, seems to mirror the mood of our electronic, instant-information world. This particular pattern might be especially appropriate in a home office.

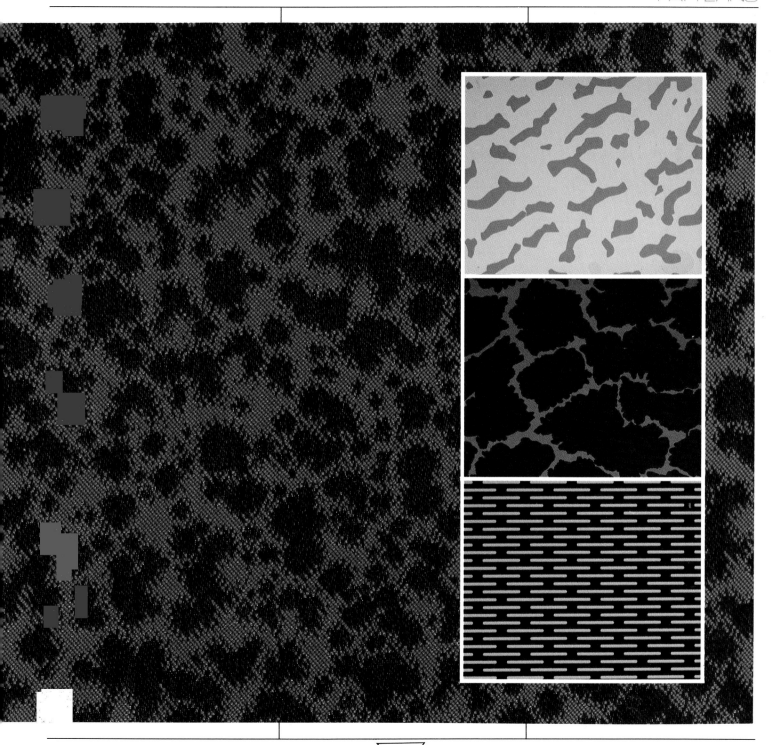

The early twentieth-century decorative design movements (whose tradition Memphis continues) aimed at an integration of decoration and architecture. For the designers who led these movements, all furniture and objects were valid on their own. They were often meant, however, to become elements of a total, unified environment, in which every detail—from the chairs to the doorknobs to the pattern on the wallpaper and the proportion of the walls—were to relate to and enhance one another. Furthermore, all these elements were created either by one person or by several working in collaboration. Many times the result of such an interrelationship would be a room in which one false move of a rug or vase guaranteed destruction of the whole. But in an atmosphere where art for art's sake was an accepted credo, such perfectly composed environments if somewhat impractical would have been praised as aesthetic successes.

Memphis, with its predilection for disunities and discontinuities, does not lay too heavy a stress on "the total Memphis" interior. True, several designers have presented hypothetical interiors, in which Memphis pieces are set against colorful, dizzyingly patterned backgrounds with clashing walls and a ceiling that clashes, in turn, with the various pieces of furniture, which, in their turn, clash with one another. Though they make their point, these rooms recall the graphics of bad (or very intense) acid trips. Accordingly, they are not exactly the sort of places in which you could live comfortably, fascinating though they are. Indeed, such interiors oppose our notion of "all the comforts of home": they are exceedingly *un*-comfortable. In place of these comforts, they offer all the chaos of the world—an aestheticized chaos, true, one that is tidied up and edited, but chaos all the same. Yet there is also something optimistic and brave about this appropriation of chaos, a willingness to accept, albeit ironically, the contemporary world as it is, a refusal to retreat to an ivory tower of "Good Design."

Given the problems such all-Memphis interiors might pose for most people, it is interesting to observe that Sottsass Associati, working along the same lines as Memphis, has created interiors that, without diluting the Memphis ideal of exuberant chaos, tone it down to a less overpowering level.

For those with no desire to live in a "total Memphis" interior of any kind, there are many possible ways of using the individual pieces in rooms decorated in various styles. To begin with, there is the notion of placing Memphis or Memphis-offshoot pieces against spare, neutral, art gallery-like backgrounds. There, they stand out like the artworks many people suppose them to be, capable of being viewed and admired from all angles. Displaying the pieces in this manner—that is, in an essentially straightfaced minimalist setting—may run counter to the Memphis notion of a design that is at once humorous and as inclusive as possible. However, some people may feel

The dining room of Rainer Krause's home features Memphis' popular "Hilton" tea trolley by Barcelona designer Javier Mariscal. Matteo Thun, one of the more well-known Memphis designers who is also one of the Sottsass Associati, created the "Sherry Netherlands" glasses and "Cuculus Canorus" teapot seen here for Anthologie Quartett, the vanguard German furniture and object manufacturer. The chair, called "Seggiolina da pranzo," is an Ettore Sottsass design offered by Studio Alchymia, the design collaborative that gave rise to Memphis.

INTERIORS

that the pieces are strong enough on their own, needing neither help nor competition from equally powerful or humorous backgrounds.

Such pure interiors might also suit those who frankly enjoy proclaiming their wealth in no uncertain terms. Uncluttered rooms with a few cunningly positioned, carefully chosen, very expensive Memphis or Memphis-like pieces will get the idea across nicely. Such careful arrangements in restrained settings will also satisfy those who like—and like their guests—to approach widely praised avant-garde furniture, no matter how irreverent, with the sort of awe usually reserved for relics of a saint.

A third approach calls for ignoring Memphis' *objet d'art* aspect altogether. Rather, the pieces are to be deployed about a room in the most casual manner possible, preferably mixed in with other designs. At first, it might seem hard to be casual about such aggressive furniture. In fact, many of the pieces do not blend in as much as they cooperate with stylistically unrelated

Burlington manufactured and Michael Volbright designed the colorful sheets that grace this bed. Bright patterns like these—more parallel to Memphis designs than directly influenced by them—can work very well in spare, otherwise patternless interiors. Note that when American companies try out Memphis-like designs, they are far more conservative than anything Memphis designers would do.

pieces—introducing a man who lives in an East End Avenue penthouse to a paramecium, for example, this juxtaposition probably will not have very much to "say" to each other, but it won't clash either. If, however, your entire living room is styled in American country, a touch of Memphis will probably look out of place. A more relaxed, more eclectic interior will accept Memphis or its offshoots more easily.

Possibly, the less big a deal you make about having this furniture in a room, the more natural it will look there. After all, Memphis is meant, at least in part, to be fun—not precious or sacred. Imagine a Memphis lamp, for example, holding its own in a room filled with books, an old sofa, some secondhand but imaginatively reupholstered club chairs, and nondescript but inoffensive end tables. No pinspot on that lamp, no space cleared away especially for it—on the contrary, it would be there just like anything

According to some designers, pristine white walls provide the most appropriate backdrop for Memphis' colorful pieces, as shown here in the Grace Designs showroom designed by Sottsass Associati and in a private residence. The white backdrops make the furniture look even more incongruous than they are. Perhaps each piece, which announces its own individuality, can be viewed as an ideal expression of what Christopher Lasch called "the culture of narcissism." Given Memphis' polyvalence, it might be that....

else, bringing with it its own associations, serving its own function, but by no means monopolizing a viewer's attention.

Used unpretentiously, a Memphis piece—or, for that matter, a Memphis plastic laminate, fabric, or rug—can serve as an unexpected but welcome visual "spicer-upper" to a room. In keeping with the anti-status outlook that underlies so many of these pieces, this use would have

us take our material possessions less, and not more, seriously. On a more poetic level, a Memphis piece might play the role of unobtrusive but supernatural visitor, the kind that one does not immediately notice as it peeks out at you from behind a stack of magazines on an autumn evening, or like a chair that under certain conditions comes to life, does whatever it has to do, and then returns to its dormant state.

While Memphis pieces are often used in spare settings, this wonderfully relaxed, old-fashioned interior in Michèle Halard's Paris house (above) incorporates several Sottsass designs—at once up-to-the-second and evocative of a slower moving time.

Among the medley of Memphis pieces in this West German home (right) are the "Columbina Descendens" teapot on the cocktail table, by Matteo Thun, and his "Sherry Netherlands" vase, for Anthologie Quartett.

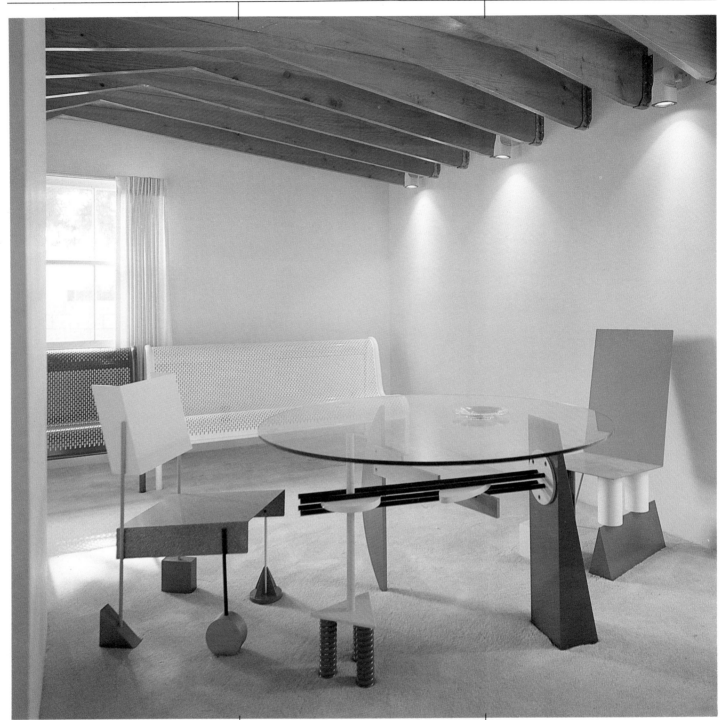

Pristine white walls (left) provide an excellent backdrop for the colorful bits and pieces that make up these Peter Shire pieces. Though Shire's pieces—and, indeed, most of Memphis' designs—rarely allude to the natural world or natural materials, it is interesting to see how well they work with the ceiling's homey exposed wood beams.

American furniture manufacturer, Thayer-Coggin, offers these pieces (right) in the "Prisma" collection, which was designed by Milo Baughman. Outlandish though they may look, the fact that both sofa and chair are—like much of the furniture Baughman designed in the fifties—raised up several inches makes them ideal for today's less-than-spacious rooms, since they have a lighter appearance than pieces that go right down to the floor.

The bright hues of the plastic-laminate-topped tables in this White Castle (right) are the sort that inspired the Memphis designers as well as Milo Baughman in his Memphis-derived "Prisma" pieces. From looking at this interior, however, and by comparing it to those shown in this chapter, you can see how designers have taken what is essentially functional but inartistic design and transformed it into an aesthetic style.

Ettore Sottsass, in an interview in 1982, noted that "fashion picks up and extracts the more immediate signals of the anthropological condition. Design picks up and redevelops on slightly longer, though not very much longer waves. But on the whole," he concludes, "everything seems to suggest that the difference in wavelengths is tending to disappear."

In fact, the cross-fertilization between Memphis and fashion (especially street and New Wave fashion) has been fairly consistent since 1981. In some instances, fashion sparked Memphis in the first place, and not vice versa. Designer Michele de Lucchi, for one, claims to have gotten a tremendous and inspiring kick out of the crowds of "punks" he saw on New Year's Eve 1980–81 in London's Trafalgar Square; indeed, New Wave patterns and graphics constitute yet another influence on this rich design style. Another influence is that of the traditional fabrics used in African garments, especially obvious in the work of Nathalie du Pasquier. In fact, du Pasquier's designs have now come full circle to the point where some of her fabric designs, originally meant for furniture and interiors, are being used in the ties and bowties Memphis offers, thereby making its own "fashion statement."

That coming-full-circle is happening on a larger scale as well. If New Wave fashion initially (if only partly) inspired Memphis, Memphis now inspires designers of clothing, jewelry, and accessories. Because the Memphis designers have thought longest and hardest about furniture, objects, and interiors, it might seem as if their ideas apply to clothing in only the most superficial way. What is a breakthrough in furni-

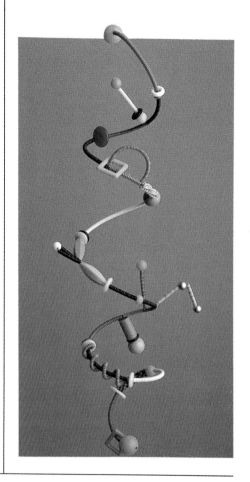

WEARABLES

"They're not planned out," says Stewart Lucas of his handpainted women's gloves. "If I've watched 'The Flintstones' on TV that day, then maybe I'll decide that everything has to look that it's made of stone." As for the television set, Lucas calls it his "trademark"—an image of the set he watched as a child.

ture design is really nothing new in fashion, where vibrant colors and busy patterns are constantly coming back into style. In fact, today's Memphis-inspired fashions do not change the face of clothing design as radically as Memphis alters the course of fur-

This earring (above), one of a pair designed by Greg Baron, is evidence of how the designer works with bright, intense color relationships within a small space. Like the fine, multicolored telephone wires out of which it is made, the earring delivers lots of information (in this case visual) in a tiny space.

Jewelry designer Greg Baron fashions earrings and bracelets from beads and telephone wire—the sort encased in gray plastic that comes in many different colors and is intended not for evening wear but for underground cables (Baron happened on the stuff in a trash can). Like Memphis designs, Baron's are, as he puts it, "playful and primitive—and very festive, good for any holiday or festive occasion."

niture and, to a lesser extent, interior design. If anything, the clothes and accessories attest to Memphis' trendiness—and to the fact that its appeal extends to people who, even if they are not in the market for a new table or lamp, would like to inject at least a small dose of Memphis into their own lives.

At present, the Memphis-inspired fashions are "fun" (if not always cheap) clothes. Memphis will lay the groundwork for a true revolution in fashion only when the clothes it inspires will be worn not merely to clubs and parties but to the straightest of offices and the most solemn of ceremonies—just as the furniture and furnishings it creates are meant to revise our notions of the straightest of rooms in people's homes, and what we do there.

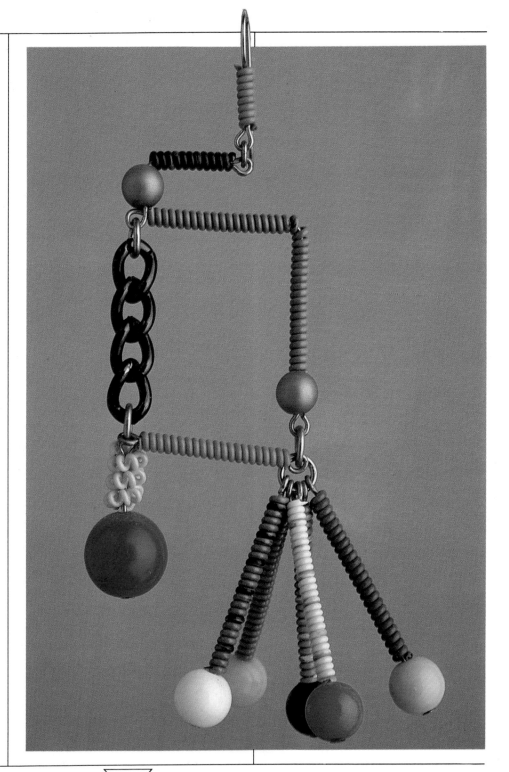

Frederico and Alfredo Viloria designed these hot-hued, sexy dresses (left), the colors of which are reminiscent of some that Memphis designers favor. The Viloria brothers were More Fashion Awards finalists. (Courtesy of More Cigarettes/R.J. Reynolds Tobacco Company)

Jewelry designer Vernon Reed's "Spaztec Warrior" pin (above) is made of anodized titanium. Like some Memphis pieces, it is a witty reminder of the sort of creatures one encounters on the screens of today's electronic games seen in arcades.

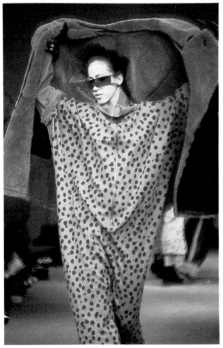

"Optique Formation Urban" is the formidable name of this dress (above) designed for Itokin by Chihiro Mirami. Its pattern, which resembles irregular paving stones, recalls some of Memphis' plastic laminate patterns. Here, though, the colors are fairly low-key; this gives the wearer an opportunity to dress in the height of fashion without having the clothing scream "fashion" at the top of its lungs. Japan's superstar fashion designer Issey Miyake spattered this flamboyant evening dress (left) with a pattern that recalls several by Memphis designers. Interestingly, Miyake has also designed a table covering, which is actually offered by Memphis itself.

Vernon Reed's colorful pieces of jewelry boast the sort of asymmetrical, jagged shapes dear to the hearts of many Memphis designers. These pieces, some of which bear the name "Memphis Calling," are made out of such unusual materials (unusual for jewelry, that is—not so unusual for, say, the rocket industry) as anodized titanium, rubber, acrylic, and liquid crystal display (LCD). Several of Reed's pieces are electronic, including "Locus Angel."

Nathalie du Pasquier designed this molded plastic brooch for Fiorucci. The little dalmatian looks as if he could have blipped out from some video game. Although du Pasquier's outlook in her fashion designs is directly related to that which informs her furniture and fabric designs, the effect with something as ephemeral and downright "cute" as this brooch is not at all intellectual or self-conscious; it's just plain fun.

Stewart Lucas' handpainted ties and gloves have patterns and colors that recall the brilliantly hued, sprayed-on graffiti you find on many subway cars in New York City. Aside from the fact that the colors and patterns partake of the Memphis mood, Lucas' graffiti suggests that this young designer reconciles the-world-as-it-is and art in much the same way that the Memphis designers do.

BIBLIOGRAPHY

Ambasz, Emilio, ed. *Italy: The New Domestic Landscape.* New York: The Museum of Modern Art, 1973.

Bayley, Stephen. "Memphis in London." London: The Boilerhouse Project, 1983.

Branzi, Andrea. "In the crisis of the industrial culture?" *Ottagono* 72 (March 1984): 68.

Breton, André. *What is Surrealism?: Selected Writings.* Edited by Franklin Rosemont. New York: Monad, 1978.

Domergue, Denise. *Artists Design Furniture.* New York: Harry N. Abrams, Inc., Publishers, 1984.

Graves, Michael. *Michael Graves, Buildings and Projects 1966–1981.* Rizzoli International Publications, Inc., 1982.

Hiesinger, Kathryn B., and George H. Marcus, eds. *Design Since 1945.* Philadelphia: Philadelphia Museum of Art, 1983.

"Is There a New Italian Style?" *Modo* (May 1981): 47.

Janjigian, Robert. "Memphis Makes It!" *Interiors,* July 1984.

MANtransFORMS. New York: The Cooper-Hewitt Museum, 1976.

"Memphis 1982" (pamphlet). Milan: Memphis, 1982.

"Memphis Furniture Milano 1983" (pamphlet). Milan: Memphis, 1983.

Nelson, George. "A Tourist's Guide to Memphis." *Interior Design* (April 1983): 214–221.

"A Passion for Fashion," *Home Furnishings Daily.* (July 23, 1984).

Penney, Richard. "The Battle of Memphis." *Industrial Design* (January–February 1983): 33–35.

Plumb, William Lansing. "Memphis on my mind." *Industrial Design* (January–February 1983): 30–32.

Radice, Barbara. *Memphis: Ricerche, esperienze, risultati, fallimenti e successi del Nuovo Design.* Milan: Electa, 1984.

Sparke, Penny. "Reflections on Memphis." London: The Boilerhouse Project, 1983.

Vercelloni, Isa. "A New International Style." *House & Garden* (February 1982): 108–117.

"Wild Beat of Memphis," *Time,* (March 26, 1984): 68–69.

SOURCES

MEMPHIS ORIGINALS

Abet Laminati
Imported by Walker & Vanger, Inc.
P.O. Box 241
Scarsdale, NY 10583

Artemide Inc.
150 East 58th St.
New York, NY

City
213 West Institute Pl.
Chicago, IL

Grace Designs
World Trade Center #622
2050 Stemmons Freeway
Dallas, TX

Janus Gallery
8000 Melrose Ave.
Los Angeles, CA

Steeles Carpets Ltd.
Boxham, Banbury, Oxon.
OX15 4HA, England

INSPIRED BY OR PARALLEL TO MEMPHIS

Atelier International
595 Madison Ave.
New York, NY

Greg Baron
137 Eighth Ave., #4
New York, NY

Susan Bennis/Warren Edwards
440 Park Ave.
New York, NY

Burlington Domestics
Burlington House
1345 Ave. of the Americas
New York, NY

USEFUL ADDRESSES

Campaniello Imports Ltd.
225 East 57th St.
New York, NY

Convergence Gallery
484 Broome St.
New York, NY

Fun Gallery
254 East 10th St.
New York, NY

The Gallery at Workbench
470 Park Ave. South
New York, NY

Gracie Mansion Gallery
337 East 10th St.
New York, NY

Hot House
345 West Broadway
New York, NY

Itokin
520 Madison Ave.
New York, NY

Knoll International
105 Wooster St.
New York, NY

George Kovacs Lighting Inc.
230 Fifth Ave.
New York, NY

Stewart Lucas
250 West 100th St.
New York, NY

Mary-James Inc.
390 Swift Ave. South
San Francisco, CA

Vincas Meilus
35 Tiffany Pl.
Brooklyn, NY

Dennis Miller Associates Inc.
72 Fifth Ave.
New York, NY

Issey Miyake USA Corp.
530 Seventh Ave.
New York, NY

Vernon Reed
4407 Sinclair Ave.
Austin, TX

Tony Shafrazi Gallery
163 Mercer St.
New York, NY

Sigma the Tastesetter
225 Fifth Ave.
New York, NY

Snyderman Gallery
317 South St.
Philadelphia, PA

Sony Corp. of America
Sony Drive
Park Ridge, NJ

Swid Powell
55 East 57th St.
New York, NY

Thayer Coggin Inc.
427 South Rd.
Box 5128
High Point, NC

The Works Gallery
319 South St.
Philadelphia, PA

David Zelman
11 Riverside Dr.
New York, NY

INDEX

INDEX

PHOTO CREDITS